MARX

THE ESSENTIAL
MARX

Karl Marx

Edited by
Leon Trotsky

Dover Publications, Inc.
Mineola, New York

Bibliographical Note

This Dover edition, first published in 2006, is an unabridged republication of *The Living Thoughts of Karl Marx,* originally published by Longmans, Green and Co., New York, in 1939. Trotsky's introductory essay was translated by Charles Malamuth. The main text of this book comes from Otto Rühle's abridgement of the first volume of *Das Kapital*; its translator into English is uncredited. The frontispiece, a woodcut portrait of Marx, was created by Professor Hans A. Mueller.

Library of Congress Cataloging-in-Publication Data

Marx, Karl, 1818–1883.
  The essential Marx / Karl Marx ; edited by Leon Trotsky.
      p. cm.
  "This Dover edition, first published in 2006, is an unabridged republication of The Living Thoughts of Karl Marx, originally published by Longmans, Green and Co., New York, in 1939" - leaf 2 of CIP galley.
  ISBN 0-486-45116-X (pbk.)
    1. Capital. 2. Economics. I. Trotsky, Leon, 1879–1940. II. Marx, Karl, 1818–1883. Living thoughts of Karl Marx. III. Title.

HB501.M3377 2006
335.4—dc22

                                                                          2006045460

Manufactured in the United States of America
Dover Publications, Inc., 31 East 2nd Street, Mineola, N.Y. 11501

MARX

KARL MARX was born May 5, 1818, at Trier, Germany, into the family of a Jewish liberal lawyer, converted to Protestantism in 1824. In the autumn of 1843 Marx moved to Paris, where he edited a revolutionary periodical and where he first met Friedrich Engels, to whom he became bound by life-long friendship. In the spring of 1847 Marx and Engels joined the clandestine Communist League. Expelled from Germany and France by the counter-revolution, Marx moved to London, where he lived with his family to the end of his days. Under his leadership the First International was founded at London in 1864. Marx's activities as a scholar were indissolubly connected with the revolutionary struggle. On March 14, 1883, seated in his working chair, Marx fell into eternal slumber. With his passing, as Engels put it, mankind became a head lower. Marx was buried in Highgate cemetery, London.

PRESENTING
KARL MARX

WHAT IS THE READER OFFERED?

This book compactly sets forth the fundamentals of Marx's economic teaching in Marx's own words. After all, no one has yet been able to expound the labor theory of value better than Marx himself.*

Certain of Marx's argumentations, especially in the first, the most difficult chapter, may seem to the uninitiated reader far too discursory, hair-splitting, or "metaphysical." As a matter of fact, this impression arises in consequence of the want of habit to approach overly habitual phenomena scientifically. The commodity has become such an all-pervasive, customary, and familiar part of our daily existence that we do not even attempt to consider why men relinquish important objects, needed to sustain life, in exchange for tiny discs of gold or silver that are of no earthly use whatever. The matter is not limited to the commodity. One and all of the categories of market economy seem to be accepted without analysis, as self-evident, as if they were the natural basis of human relations. Yet, while the realities of the economic process are human labor, raw materials, tools, machines, division of labor,

* The abridgement of the first volume of *Capital* — the foundation of Marx's entire system of economics — was made by Mr. Otto Rühle with profound understanding of his task. First to be eliminated were obsolete examples, then quotations from writings which today are only of historic interest, polemics with writers now forgotten, and finally numerous documents which, whatever their importance for understanding a given epoch, have no place in a concise exposition that pursues theoretical rather than historical objectives. At the same time, Mr. Rühle did everything to preserve continuity in the development of the scientific analysis. Logical deductions and dialectic transitions of thought have not, we trust, been infringed at any point. It stands to reason that this extract calls for attentive perusal.

the necessity to distribute finished products among the participants of the labor process, and the like, such categories as "commodity," "money," "wages," "capital," "profit," "tax," and the like are only semi-mystical reflections in men's heads of the various aspects of a process of economy which they do not understand and which is not under their control. To decipher them, a thoroughgoing scientific analysis is indispensable.

In the United States, where a man who owns a million is referred to as being "worth" a million, market concepts have sunk in deeper than anywhere else. Until quite recently Americans gave very little thought to the nature of economic relations. In the land of the most powerful economic system economic theory continued to be exceedingly barren. Only the present deep-going crisis of American economy has bluntly confronted public opinion with the fundamental problems of capitalist society. In any event, whoever has not overcome the habit of uncritically accepting the ready-made ideological reflections of economic development, whoever has not reasoned out, in the footsteps of Marx, the essential nature of the commodity as the basic cell of the capitalist organism, will prove to be forever incapable of scientifically comprehending the most important manifestations of our epoch.

MARX'S METHOD

Having established science as cognition of the objective recurrences of nature, man has tried stubbornly and persistently to exclude himself from science, reserving for himself special privileges in the shape of alleged intercourse with supersensory forces (religion), or with timeless moral precepts (idealism). Marx deprived man of these odious privileges definitely and forever, looking upon him as a natural link in the evolutionary process of material nature ; upon human society as the organization of production and distribution ; upon capitalism as a stage in the development of human society.

It was not Marx's aim to discover the "eternal laws" of economy. He denied the existence of such laws. The history of the development of human society is the history of the succession of various systems of economy, each operating in accordance with its own laws. The transition from one system to another was always determined by the growth of the productive forces, i. e., of technique and the organization of labor. Up to a certain point, social changes are quantitative in character and do not alter the foundations of society, i. e., the prevalent forms of property. But a point is reached when the matured productive forces can no longer contain themselves within the old forms of property ; then follows a radical change in the social order, accompanied by shocks. The primitive commune was either superseded or supplemented by slavery ; slavery was succeeded by serfdom with its feudal superstructure ; the commercial development of cities brought Europe in the sixteenth century to the capitalist order, which thereupon passed through several stages. In his *Capital* Marx does not study economy in general, but *capitalist* economy, which has its own specific laws. Only in passing does he refer to other economic systems, to elucidate the characteristics of capitalism.

The self-sufficient economy of the primitive peasant family has no need of a "political economy," for it is dominated on the one hand by the forces of nature and on the other by the forces of tradition. The self-contained natural economy of the Greeks or the Romans, founded on slave labor, was ruled by the will of the slave-owner, whose "plan" in turn was directly determined by the laws of nature and routine. The same might also be said about the medieval estate with its peasant serfs. In all these instances economic relations were clear and transparent in their primitive crudity. But the case of contemporary society is altogether different. It destroyed the old self-contained connections and the inherited modes of labor. The new economic

KARL MARX

nations. Division of labor has encompassed the planet.
Having shattered tradition and routine, these bonds
have not composed themselves according to some definite plan, but rather apart from human consciousness
and foresight. The interdependence of men, groups,
classes, nations, which follows from division of labor, is
not directed by anyone. People work for each other
without knowing each other, without inquiring about
one another's needs, in the hope, and even with the
assurance, that their relations will somehow regulate
themselves. And by and large they do, or rather, were
wont to.

It is utterly impossible to seek the causes for the recurrences in capitalist society in the subjective consciousness — in the intentions or plans — of its members.
The objective recurrences of capitalism were formulated before science began to think about them seriously.
To this day the preponderant majority of men know
nothing about the laws that govern capitalist economy.
The whole strength of Marx's method was in his approach to economic phenomena, not from the subjective point of view of certain persons, but from the objective point of view of the development of society as
a whole, just as an experimental natural scientist ap-
proaches a beehive or an ant-hill.

For economic science the decisive significance is what
and how people act, not what they themselves think
about their actions. At the base of society is not religion
and morality, but nature and labor. Marx's method is
materialistic, because it proceeds from existence to consciousness, not the other way around. Marx's method is
dialectic, because it regards both nature and society as
they evolve, and evolution itself as the constant struggle
of conflicting forces.

MARXISM AND OFFICIAL SCIENCE

Marx had his predecessors. Classical political economy — Adam Smith, David Ricardo — reached its full bloom before capitalism had grown old, before it began to fear the morrow. Marx paid to both great classicists the perfect tribute of profound gratitude. Nevertheless the basic error of classical economics was its view of capitalism as humanity's normal existence for all time instead of merely as one historical stage in the development of society. Marx began with a criticism of that political economy, exposed its errors, as well as the contradictions of capitalism itself, and demonstrated the inevitability of its collapse.

Science does not reach its goal in the hermetically sealed study of the scholar, but in flesh-and-blood society. All the interests and passions that rend society asunder exert their influence on the development of science — especially of political economy, the science of wealth and poverty. The struggle of workers against capitalists forced the theoreticians of the bourgeoisie to turn their backs upon a scientific analysis of the system of exploitation and to busy themselves with a bare description of economic facts, a study of the economic past and, what is immeasurably worse, a downright falsification of things as they are for the purpose of justifying the capitalist regime. The economic doctrine which is nowadays taught in official institutions of learning and preached in the bourgeois press offers no dearth of important factual material, yet it is utterly incapable of encompassing the economic process as a whole and discovering its laws and perspectives, nor has it any desire to do so. Official political economy is dead.

THE LAW OF LABOR VALUE

In contemporary society man's cardinal tie is exchange. Any product of labor that enters into the process of exchange becomes a commodity. Marx began his investigation with the commodity and deduced from that fundamental cell of capitalist society those social relations that have objectively shaped themselves on the basis of exchange, independently of man's will. Only by pursuing this course is it possible to solve the fundamental puzzle — how in capitalist society, in which each man thinks for himself and no one thinks for all, are created the relative proportions of the various branches of economy indispensable to life.

The worker sells his labor power, the farmer takes his produce to the market, the money lender or banker grants loans, the storekeeper offers an assortment of merchandise, the industrialist builds a plant, the speculator buys and sells stocks and bonds — each having his own considerations, his own private plan, his own concern about wages or profit. Nevertheless, out of this chaos of individual strivings and actions emerges a certain economic whole, which, true, is not harmonious, but contradictory, yet does give society the possibility not merely to exist but even to develop. This means that, after all, chaos is not chaos at all, that in some way it is regulated automatically, if not consciously. To understand the mechanism whereby various aspects of economy are brought into a state of relative balance, is to discover the objective laws of capitalism.

Clearly, the laws which govern the various spheres of capitalist economy — wages, price, land rent, profit, interest, credit, the stock exchange — are numerous and complex. But in the final reckoning they come down to the single law that Marx discovered and explored to the end ; that is, *the law of labor value*, which is indeed the basic regulator of capitalist economy. The essence of that law is simple. Society has at its disposal a certain reserve of living labor power. Applied to nature, that power produces products necessary for the satisfaction of human needs. In consequence of division of labor among independent producers, the products assume the form of commodities. Commodities are exchanged for each other in a given ratio, at first directly, and eventually through the medium of gold or money. The basic property of commodities, which in a certain relationship makes them equal to each other, is the human labor expended upon them — abstract labor, labor in general — the basis and the measure of value. Division of labor among millions of scattered producers does not lead to the disintegration of society, because commodities are exchanged according to the socially necessary labor time expended upon them. By accepting and rejecting commodities, the market, as the arena of exchange, decides whether they do or do not contain within themselves socially necessary labor, thereby determines the ratios of the various kinds of commodities necessary for society, and consequently also the distribution of labor power according to the various trades.

The actual processes of the market are immeasurably more complex than has been here set forth in but a few lines. Thus, oscillating around the value of labor, prices fluctuate above and below their values. The causes of these deviations are fully explained in the third volume of Marx's *Capital*, which describes "the process of capitalist production considered as a whole." Nevertheless, great as may be the divergences between the prices and the values of commodities in individual instances, the sum of all prices is equal to the sum of all values, for in the final reckoning only the values that have been created by human labor are at the disposal of society, and prices cannot break through this limitation, including even the monopoly prices of trusts ; where labor has created no new value, there even Rockefeller can get nothing.

INEQUALITY AND EXPLOITATION

But if commodities are exchanged for each other according to the quantity of labor invested in them, how does inequality come out of equality ? Marx solved this puzzle by exposing the peculiar nature of one of the commodities, which lies at the basis of all other commodities : namely, labor power. The owner of means of production, the capitalist, buys labor power. Like all other commodities, it is evaluated according to the quantity of labor invested in it, i. e., of those means of subsistence which are necessary for the survival and the reproduction of the worker. But the consumption of that commodity — labor power — consists of work, i. e., the creation of new values. The quantity of these values is greater than those which the worker himself receives and which he expends for his upkeep. The capitalist buys labor power in order to exploit it. It is this exploitation which is the source of inequality.

That part of the product which goes to cover the worker's own subsistence Marx calls *necessary*-produce ; that part which the worker produces above this, is *surplus*-produce. Surplus-produce must have been produced by the slave, or the slave-owner would not have kept any slaves. Surplus-produce must have been produced by the serf, or serfdom would have been of no use to the landed gentry. Surplus-produce, only to a considerably greater extent, is likewise produced by the wage worker, or the capitalist would have no need to buy labor power. The class struggle is nothing else than the struggle for surplus-produce. He who owns surplus-produce is master of the situation — owns wealth, owns the state, has the key to the church, to the courts, to the sciences, and to the arts.

COMPETITION AND MONOPOLY

Relations amongst capitalists, who exploit the workers, are determined by competition, which for long endures as the mainspring of capitalist progress. Large enterprises enjoy technical, financial, organizational, economic and, last but not least, political advantages over small enterprises. The greater amount of capital, being able to exploit a greater number of workers, inevitably emerges victorious out of a contest. Such is the unalterable basis of the concentration and centralization process of capital.

While stimulating the progressive development of

technique, competition gradually consumes, not only the intermediary layers, but itself as well. Over the corpses and semi-corpses of small and middling capitalists emerges an ever-decreasing number of ever more powerful capitalist overlords. Thus, out of *honest, democratic, progressive* competition grows irrevocably *harmful, parasitic, reactionary* monopoly. Its sway began to assert itself in the eighties of the past century, assuming definite shape at the turn of the present century. Now the victory of monopoly is openly acknowledged by the most official representatives of bourgeois society.* Yet when in the course of his prognosis Marx had first deduced monopoly from the inherent tendencies of capitalism, the bourgeois world had looked upon competition as an eternal law of nature.

The elimination of competition by monopoly marks the beginning of the disintegration of capitalist society. Competition was the creative mainspring of capitalism and the historical justification of the capitalist. By the same token the elimination of competition marks the transformation of stockholders into social parasites. Competition had to have certain liberties, a liberal atmosphere, a regime of democracy, of commercial cosmopolitanism. Monopoly needs as authoritative a government as possible, tariff walls, "its own" sources of raw materials and arenas of marketing (colonies). The last word in the distintegration of monopolistic capital is *Fascism.*

CONCENTRATION OF WEALTH AND THE GROWTH OF CLASS CONTRADICTIONS

Capitalists and their advocates try in every way to hide the real extent of the concentration of wealth from the eyes of the people as well as from the eyes of the tax

* Competition as a restraining influence, complains the former Attorney General of the United States, Mr. Homer S. Cummings, is being gradually displaced and, in large fields, remains only "as a shadowy reminder of conditions that once existed."

collector. In defiance of the obvious, the bourgeois press is still attempting to maintain the illusion of a "democratic" distribution of capital investment. The New York *Times*, in refutation of the Marxists, points out that there are from three to five million separate employers of labor. Joint-stock companies, it is true, represent greater concentration of capital than three to five million separate employers, yet the United States does have "half a million corporations." This sort of trifling with lump sums and average figures is resorted to, not in order to disclose, but in order to hide things as they are.

From the beginning of the war until 1923 the number of plants and factories in the United States fell from index figure 100 to 98.7, while the mass of industrial production rose from 100 to 156.3. During the years of sensational prosperity (1923–1929), when it seemed that everybody was getting rich, the number of establishments fell from 100 to 93.8, while production rose from 100 to 113. Yet the concentration of business establishments, bound by their ponderous material bodies, is far behind the concentration of their souls, i. e., ownership. In 1929 the United States did actually have more than 300,000 corporations, as the New York *Times* correctly observes. It is only necessary to add that 200 of these, i. e., 0.07 percent of the entire number, directly controlled 49.2 percent of the assets of all the corporations. Four years later that ratio had already risen to 56 percent, while during the years of Roosevelt's administration it has undoubtedly risen still higher. Inside these 200 leading joint-stock companies the actual domination belongs to a small minority.*

---

* A committee of the United States Senate found out in February 1937, that for the past twenty years the decisions of twelve of the very largest corporations have been tantamount to directives for the greater part of American industry. The number of chairmen of the board of these corporations is about the same

The same processes may be observed in the banking and insurance systems. Five of the largest insurance companies in the United States have absorbed not only the other companies but even many banks. The total number of banks is reduced, chiefly in the form of so-called "mergers," essentially by being absorbed. The extent of the turnover grows rapidly. Above the banks rises the oligarchy of super-banks. Bank capital merges with industrial capital into financial super-capital. Supposing that the concentration of industry and banks were to proceed at the same rate as during the last quarter of a century — as a matter of fact, the tempo of concentration is on the increase — in the course of the impending quarter century the monopolists will have garnered unto themselves the entire economy of the country, without leaving over as much as the widow's mite.

The statistics of the United States are here resorted to only because they are more exact and more striking. Essentially the process of concentration is international in character. Throughout the various stages of capitalism, through phases of conjunctural cycles, through all the political regimes, through peaceful periods as well as through periods of armed conflicts, the process of the concentration of all the great fortunes into an ever-decreasing number of hands has gone on and will continue without end. During the years of the Great War, when the nations were bleeding to death, when the very bodies politic of the bourgeoisie lay crushed under the weight of national debts, when fiscal systems rolled into the abyss, dragging the middle classes after them, the monopolists were coining unprecedented profits out of the blood and muck. The most powerful com-

---

as the number of members in the cabinet of the President of the United States, the executive branch of the republic's government. But these chairmen of the board are immeasurably more powerful than the cabinet members.

panies of the United States increased their assets during
the years of the war two, three, four and more times
and swelled their dividends to 300, 400, 900 and more
percent.

In 1840, eight years before the publication by Marx
and Engels of the Manifesto of the Communist Party,
the famous French writer Alexis de Tocqueville wrote
in his book *Democracy in America* : "Great wealth
tends to disappear, the number of small fortunes to increase." That thought has been reiterated innumerable
times, at first with reference to the United States, later
with reference to those other young democracies, Australia and New Zealand. Of course, de Tocqueville's
view was already erroneous in his own day. Still, real
concentration of wealth began only after the American
Civil War, on the eve of which de Tocqueville died.
At the beginning of the present century two percent of
the population of the United States already owned more
than half of the entire wealth of the country ; in 1929
the same two percent owned three-fifths of the national
wealth. At the same time, 36,000 wealthy families had
as great an income as 11,000,000 middling and poor families. During the crisis of 1929–1933 monopolistic establishments had no need to appeal to public charity ; on
the contrary, they rose higher than ever above the general decline of national economy. During the ensuing
rickety industrial revival on the yeast-cakes of the New
Deal the monopolists again skimmed a lot of heavy
cream. The number of the unemployed decreased at
best from 20,000,000 to 10,000,000 ; at the same time the
upper crust of capitalist society — no more than 6000
adults — garnered fantastic dividends ; this is what So-
licitor General Robert H. Jackson proved with figures
during his tenure as Anti-Trust Assistant Attorney General of the United States.

But, the abstract concept, "monopolistic capital," is
filled in for us with flesh and blood. What it means is

that a handful of families,* bound by ties of kinship and common interest into an exclusive capitalist oligarchy, dispose of the economic and political fortunes of a great nation. One must perforce admit that the Marxist law of concentration has worked out famously !

HAS MARX'S TEACHING BECOME OBSOLETE ?

Questions of competition, concentration of wealth, and monopoly naturally lead to the question whether in our day Marx's economic theory is merely of historic interest — as, for example, Adam Smith's theory — or whether it continues to be of actual significance. The criterion for replying to that question is simple : if the theory correctly estimates the course of development and foresees the future better than other theories, it remains the most advanced theory of our time, be it even scores of years old.

The famous German economist, Werner Sombart, who was virtually a Marxist at the beginning of his career but later revised all the more revolutionary aspects of Marx's teaching, countered Marx's *Capital* with his own *Capitalism*, which probably is the best known exposition of bourgeois economic apologetics in recent times. Sombart wrote : "Karl Marx prophesied : firstly, the increasing misery of hired workers ; secondly, general 'concentration,' with the disappearance of the class of artisans and peasants ; thirdly, the catastrophic collapse

* The American writer Ferdinand Lundberg who, for all his scholarly conscientiousness, is a rather conservative economist, wrote in his book, which created quite a stir : "The United States is owned and dominated today by a hierarchy of sixty of the richest families, buttressed by no more than ninety families of lesser wealth." To these might be added a third tier of perhaps three hundred and fifty other families, with incomes in excess of a hundred thousand dollars a year. The predominant position there belongs to the first group of sixty families, who dominate not only the market but all the levers of government. They are the real government, "the government of money in a dollar democracy."

of capitalism. Nothing of the kind has come to pass."

Against this erroneous prognosis Sombart counter-poses his own "strictly scientific" prognosis. "Capital-ism will continue," according to him, "to transform itself internally in the same direction in which it has already begun to transform itself, at the time of its apogee : as it grows older, it will become more and more calm, sedate, reasonable." Let us try to verify, if only along the basic lines, which of the two is right : Marx, with his prognosis of catastrophe, or Sombart, who in the name of all bourgeois economy promised that matters would be adjusted "calmly, sedately, rea-sonably." The reader will agree that the question is worthy of notice.

A. *"The Theory of Increasing Misery"*

"Accumulation of wealth at one pole," wrote Marx sixty years before Sombart, "is, therefore, at the same time accumulation of misery, agony of toil, slavery, ignorance, brutality, mental degradation, at the oppo-site pole, i. e., on the side of the class that produces its product in the form of capital." That thesis of Marx's, under the name of "The Theory of Increasing Misery," has been subjected to constant attacks by democratic and social-democratic reformers, especially during the period 1896–1914, when capitalism developed rapidly and yielded certain concessions to the workers, espe-cially to their upper stratum. After the World War, when the bourgeoisie, frightened by its own crimes and by the October Revolution, took to the road of adver-tised social reforms, the value of which was simultane-ously nullified by inflation and unemployment, the theory of the progressive transformation of capitalist society seemed to the reformers and to the bourgeois professors fully warranted. "The purchasing power of hired labor," Sombart assured us in 1928, "has increased in direct ratio to the expansion of capitalist production."

As a matter of fact, the economic contradiction be-

tween the proletariat and the bourgeoisie was aggra-
vated during the most prosperous periods of capitalist
development, when the rise in the standard of living of
certain strata of toilers, which at times were rather extensive, hid the decrease of the proletariat's share in the
national income. Thus, just before falling into prostration, the industrial production of the United States, for
instance, increased by 50 percent between 1920 and
1930, while the sum paid out in wages rose only by 30
percent, which meant a tremendous decrease of labor's
share in the national income. In 1930 began an ominous
growth of unemployment, and in 1933 a more or less
systematic aid to the unemployed, who received in the
form of relief hardly more than one half of what they
had lost in the form of wages. The illusion of the uninterrupted "progress" of all classes has vanished without
a trace. The *relative* decline of the masses' standard of
living has been superseded by an *absolute* decline.
Workers begin by economizing on skimpy entertainment, then on their clothes and finally on their food.
Articles and products of average quality are superseded
by shoddy ones, and the shoddy by the worst. Trade
unions begin to look like the man who hangs on des-
perately to the handrail while going down in a rapidly
descending escalator.

With six percent of the world's population, the
United States holds forty percent of the world's wealth.
Still, one third of the nation, as Roosevelt himself ad-
mits, is undernourished, inadequately clothed, and lives
under subhuman conditions. What is there to say, then,
for the far less privileged countries ? The history of the
capitalist world since the last war has irrefutably borne
out the so-called "theory of increasing misery."

The Fascist regime, which merely reduces to the utmost the limits of decline and reaction inherent in any
imperialist capitalism, became indispensable when the
degeneration of capitalism blotted out the possibility
of maintaining illusions about a rise in the proletariat's

standard of living. Fascist dictatorship means the open acknowledgement of the tendency to impoverishment, which the wealthier imperialist democracies are still trying to disguise. Mussolini and Hitler persecute Marxism with such hatred precisely because their own regime is the most horrible confirmation of the Marxist prognosis. The civilized world was indignant or pretended to be indignant when Goering, in the tone of the executioner and buffoon peculiar to him, declared that guns were more important than butter, or when Cagliostro-Casanova-Mussolini advised the workers of Italy to learn to pull in tighter the belts on their black shirts. But does not substantially the same take place in the imperialist democracies? Butter everywhere is used to grease guns. The workers of France, England, the United States learn to pull in their belts without having black shirts.

B. *The Reserve Army and the New Sub-Class of the Unemployed*

The industrial reserve army makes up an indispensable component part of the social mechanics of capitalism, as much as a supply of machines and raw materials in factory warehouses or of finished products in stores. Neither the general expansion of production nor the adaptation of capital to the periodic ebb and flow of the industrial cycle would be possible without a reserve of labor-power. From the general tendency of capitalist development — the increase of constant capital (machines and raw materials) at the expense of variable capital (labor-power) — Marx drew the conclusion: "The greater the social wealth . . . the greater is the industrial reserve army . . . the greater is the mass of a consolidated surplus-population . . . the greater is official pauperism. *This is the absolute general law of capitalist accumulation.*"

That thesis — indissolubly bound up with the "theory of increasing misery" and for scores of years denounced as "exaggerated," "tendentious," and "demagogic" — has now become the irreproachable theoretical image of things as they are. The present army of unemployed can no longer be regarded as a "reserve army," because its basic mass can no longer have any hope of returning to employment; on the contrary, it is bound to be swelled by a constant flow of additional unemployed. Disintegrating capitalism has brought up a whole generation of young people who have never had a job and have no hope of getting one. This new sub-class between the proletariat and the semi-proletariat is forced to live at the expense of society. It has been estimated that in the course of nine years (1930–1938) unemployment has taken out of the economy of the United States more than 43,000,000 labor man-years. Considering that in 1929, at the height of prosperity, there were two million unemployed in the United States and that during those nine years the number of potential workers has increased by five million, the total number of lost man-years must be incomparably higher. A social regime ravaged by such a plague is sick unto death. The proper diagnosis of this malady was made nearly four score of years ago, when the disease itself was a mere germ.

C. *The Decline of the Middle Classes*

Figures which demonstrate the concentration of capital indicate therewith that the specific gravity of the middle class in production and its share of the national income have been constantly declining, while small holdings have either been completely swallowed up or reduced in grade and robbed of their independence, becoming a mere badge of unendurable toil and desperate want. At the same time, it is true, the development of capitalism has considerably stimulated an increase in the army of technicians, managers, servicemen, clerks, attorneys, physicians — in a word, of the so-called "new middle class." But that stratum, the growth of which was already no mystery even to Marx, has little in common with the old middle class, who in the ownership of its own means of production had a tangible guarantee of economic independence. The "new middle class" is more directly dependent on the capitalists than are the workers. Indeed, the middle class is in large measure their taskmaster. Moreover, among it has been noticed considerable overproduction, with its aftermath of social degradation.

"Reliable statistical information," states a person as remote from Marxism as the already-quoted former Attorney General of the United States Homer S. Cummings, "shows that very many industrial units have completely disappeared and that what took place was a progressive elimination of the small business man as a factor in American life." But, objects Sombart, "general concentration, with the disappearance of the class of artisans and peasants," has not yet taken place. Like every theoretician, Marx began by isolating the fundamental tendencies in their pure form ; otherwise, it would have been altogether impossible to understand the destiny of capitalist society. Marx himself was, however, perfectly capable of viewing the phenomena of life in the light of concrete analysis, as a product of the concatenation of diverse historical factors. Surely, Newton's laws are not invalidated by the fact that the rate of speed in the fall of bodies varies under different conditions or that the orbits of planets are subjected to disturbances.

In order to understand the so-called "tenacity" of the middle classes, it is well to bear in mind that the two tendencies, the ruination of the middle classes and the transformation of these ruined ones into proletarians, develop neither at an even pace nor to the same extent. It follows from the increasing preponderance of the machine over labor-power that the further the process of the ruination of the middle classes proceeds, the more it outstrips the process of their proletarianization ; in-

deed, at a certain juncture the latter must cease altogether and even back up.

Just as the operation of the laws of physiology yields
different results in a growing organism from those in
a dying one, so the economic laws of Marxist economy
assert themselves differently in a developing and a disintegrating capitalism. This difference is shown with
especial clarity in the mutual relations of town and
country. The rural population of the United States,
increasing comparatively at a slower rate than the total
population, continued to increase in absolute figures until 1910, when it amounted to more than 32,000,000.
During the subsequent twenty years, notwithstanding
the rapid increase in the country's total population, it
fell to 30.4 millions, i. e., by 1.6 millions. But in 1935
it rose again to 32.8 millions, swelling in comparison
with 1930 by 2.4 millions. This turn of the wheel, as-
tonishing at first glance, does not in the least refute
either the tendency of the urban population to increase
at the expense of the rural population, or the tendency
of the middle classes to become atomized, while at the
same time it demonstrates most pointedly the disintegration of the capitalist system as a whole. The increase in
the rural population during the period of the acute crisis
of 1930–1935 is simply explained by the fact that well-
nigh two million of urban population, or, speaking more
to the point, two million of starving unemployed, moved
into the country — to plots of land abandoned by farmers or to the farms of their kith and kin, so as to apply
their labor-power, rejected by society, to productive
natural economy and in order to drag out a semi-starved
existence instead of starving altogether.

Hence, it is not a question of the stability of small
farmers, artisans, and store-keepers, but rather of the
abject helplessness of their situation. Far from being a
guarantee of the future, the middle class is an unfortunate and tragic relic of the past. Unable to stamp it out
altogether, capitalism has managed to reduce it to the

utmost degree of degradation and distress. The farmer is denied, not only the rent due him for his plot of land and the profit on his invested capital, but even a goodly portion of his wages. Similarly, the little fellows in town fret out their allotted span between economic life and death. The middle class is not proletarianized only because it is pauperized. In that it is just as hard to find an argument against Marx as in favor of capitalism.

D. *Industrial Crises*

The end of the past and the beginning of the present century were marked by such overwhelming progress made by capitalism that cyclical crises seemed to be no more than "accidental" annoyances. During the years of almost universal capitalist optimism, Marx's critics assured us that the national and international development of trusts, syndicates, and cartels introduced planned control of the market and presaged the final triumph over crises. According to Sombart, crises had already been "abolished" before the war by the mechanics of capitalism itself, so that "the problem of crises leaves us today virtually indifferent." Now, a mere ten years later, these words sound like hollow mockery, while only in our own day does Marx's prognosis loom in the full measure of its tragic cogency.

It is remarkable that the capitalist press, which half-way tries to deny the very existence of monopolies, resorts to these same monopolies in order half-way to deny capitalistic anarchy. If sixty families were to control the economic life of the United States, the New York *Times* observes ironically, "it would show that American capitalism, so far from being 'anarchic' and 'planless' . . . is organized with great neatness." This argument misses the mark. Capitalism has been unable to develop a single one of its trends to the ultimate end. Just as the concentration of wealth does not abolish the middle class, so monopoly does not abolish competition, but only bears down on it and mangles it. No less than the "plan" of each of the sixty families, the sundry variants of these plans are not in the least interested in coordinating the various branches of economy, but rather in increasing the profits of their own monopolistic clique at the expense of other cliques and at the expense of the entire nation. The crossing of such plans in the final reckoning only deepens the anarchy in the national economy.

The crisis of 1929 broke out in the United States one year after Sombart had proclaimed the utter indifference of his "science" to the very problem of crises. From the peak of unprecedented prosperity the economy of the United States was catapulted into the abyss of monstrous prostration. No one in Marx's day could have conceived convulsions of such magnitude ! The national income of the United States had risen for the first time in 1920 to sixty-nine billion dollars, only to drop the very next year to fifty billion dollars, i. e., by 27%. In consequence of the prosperity of the next few years, the national income rose again, in 1929, to its highest point of eighty-one billion dollars, only to drop in 1932 to forty billion dollars, i. e., by more than half ! During the nine years 1930–1938 were lost approximately forty-three million man-years of labor and 133 billion dollars of the national income, assuming the norms of labor and income of 1929, when there were "only" two million unemployed. If all this is not anarchy, what can possibly be the meaning of that word ?

E. *The "Theory of Collapse"*

The minds and hearts of middle-class intellectuals and trade-union bureaucrats were almost completely enthralled by the achievements of capitalism between the time of Marx's death and the outbreak of the World War. The idea of gradual progress ("evolution") seemed to have been made secure for all time, while the idea of revolution was regarded as a mere relic of barbarism. Marx's prognosis was countered with the

qualitatively contrary prognosis about the more bal-
anced distribution of the national income, about the
softening of class contradictions, and about the gradual
reformation of capitalist society. Jean Jaurès, the most
gifted of the Social Democrats of that classic epoch,
hoped gradually to fill political democracy with social
content. In that lay the essence of reformism. Such
was the alternative prognosis. What is left of it?

The life of monopolistic capitalism in our time is a
chain of crises. Each crisis is a catastrophe. The need
of salvation from these partial catastrophes by means
of tariff walls, inflation, increase of government spend-
ing, and debts lays the ground for additional, deeper, and
more widespread crises. The struggle for markets, for
raw materials, for colonies makes military catastrophes
unavoidable. All in all, they prepare revolutionary catastrophes. Truly, it is not easy to agree with Sombart
that aging capitalism becomes increasingly "calm, sedate and reasonable." It would be more apt to say that
it is losing its last vestiges of reason. In any event, there
is no doubt that the "theory of collapse" has triumphed
over the theory of peaceful development.

THE DECAY OF CAPITALISM

However expensive the control of the market has
been to society, mankind up to a certain stage, approximately until the World War, grew, developed, and en-
riched itself through partial and general crises. The
private ownership of the means of production continued
to be in that epoch a comparatively progressive factor.
But now the blind control by the law of value refuses
to render further service. Human progress is stuck in
a blind alley. Notwithstanding the latest triumphs of
technical thought, the material productive forces are
no longer growing. The clearest symptom of the decline is the world stagnation in the building industry, in
consequence of the stoppage of new investments in the
basic branches of economy. Capitalists are simply no

longer able to believe in the future of their own system. Constructions stimulated by the government means a rise in taxation and the contraction of the "untrammelled" national income, especially since the main part of the new government constructions is directly designed for war purposes.

The marasmus has acquired a particularly degrading character in the most ancient sphere of human activity, the one most closely connected with the basic vital needs of man — in agriculture. No longer satisfied with the obstacles which private ownership in its most reactionary form, that of small landholdings, places before the development of agriculture, capitalist governments see themselves not infrequently called upon to limit production artificially with the aid of statutory and administrative measures which would have frightened artisans in the guilds at the time of their decline. It will be recorded in history that the government of the most powerful capitalist country granted premiums to farmers for cutting down on their planting, i. e., for artificially diminishing the already falling national income. The results are self-evident : despite grandiose productive possibilities, secured by experience and science, agrarian economy does not emerge from a putrescent crisis, while the number of the hungry, the preponderant majority of mankind, continues to increase faster than the population of our planet. Conservatives consider it sensible politics to defend a social order which has descended to such destructive madness and they condemn the Socialist fight against such madness as destructive Utopianism.

FASCISM AND THE NEW DEAL

Two methods for saving historically doomed capitalism are today vying with each other in the world arena — Fascism and the New Deal. Fascism bases its program on the demolition of labor organizations, on the destruction of social reforms, and on the complete annihilation of democratic rights, in order to forestall a resurrection of the proletariat's class struggle. The Fascist state officially legalizes the degradation of workers and the pauperization of the middle classes, in the name of saving the "nation" and the "race" — presumptuous names under which decaying capitalism figures.

The policy of the New Deal, which tries to save imperialist democracy by way of sops to the labor and farmer aristocracy, is in its broad compass accessible only to the very wealthy nations, and so in that sense it is American policy *par excellence*. The American government has attempted to shift a part of the costs of that policy to the shoulders of the monopolists, exhorting them to raise wages and shorten the labor day and thus increase the purchasing power of the population and extend production. Léon Blum attempted to translate this sermon into elementary school French. In vain ! The French capitalist, like the American, does not produce for the sake of production but for profit. He is always ready to limit production, even to destroy manufactured products, if thereby his own share of the national income will be increased.

The New Deal program is all the more inconsistent in that, while preaching sermons to the magnates of capital about the advantages of abundance over scarcity, the government dispenses premiums for cutting down on production. Is greater confusion possible ? The government confutes its critics with the challenge : can you do better ? What all this means is that on the basis of capitalism the situation is hopeless.

Beginning with 1933, i. e., in the course of the last six years in America, the federal government, the states, and the municipalities have handed out to the unemployed nearly fifteen billion dollars in relief, a sum quite insufficient in itself and representing merely the smaller part of lost wages, but at the same time, considering the declining national income, a colossal sum. During 1938, which was a year of comparative economic revival, the national debt of the United States increased by two billion dollars past the thirty-eight billion dollar mark, or twelve billion dollars more than the highest point at the end of the World War. Early in 1939 it passed the forty billion dollar mark. And then what ? The mounting national debt is of course a burden on posterity. But the New Deal itself was possible only because of the tremendous wealth accumulated by past generations. Only a very rich nation could indulge itself in so extravagant a policy. But even such a nation cannot indefinitely go on living at the expense of past generations. The New Deal policy with its fictitious achievements and its very real increase in the national debt is unavoidably bound to culminate in ferocious capitalist reaction and a devastating explosion of imperialism. In other words, it is directed into the same channels as the policy of Fascism.

ANOMALY OR NORM ?

The Secretary of the Interior of the United States, Harold L. Ickes, considers it "one of the strangest anomalies in all history" that America, democratic in form, is autocratic in substance : "America, the land of majority rule but controlled at least until 1933 (!) by monopolies that in their turn are controlled by a negligible number of their stockholders." The diagnosis is correct, with the exception of the intimation that with the advent of Roosevelt the rule of monopoly either ceased or weakened. Yet what Ickes calls "one of the strangest anomalies in all history," is, as a matter of fact, the unquestionable norm of capitalism. The domination of the weak by the strong, of the many by the few, of the toilers by the exploiters is a basic law of bourgeois democracy. What distinguishes the United States from other countries is merely the greater scope and the greater heinousness in the contradictions of its capitalism. The absence of a feudal past, rich natural resources, an energetic and enterprising people, in a word, all the pre-requisites that augured an uninterrupted development of democracy, have actually brought about a fantastic concentration of wealth.

Promising this time to wage the fight against monopolies to a triumphant issue, Ickes recklessly harks back to Thomas Jefferson, Andrew Jackson, Abraham Lincoln, Theodore Roosevelt, and Woodrow Wilson as the predecessors of Franklin D. Roosevelt. "Practically all of our greatest historical figures," said he on December 30, 1937, "are famous because of their persistent and courageous fight to prevent and control the overconcentration of wealth and power in a few hands." But it follows from his own words that the fruit of this "persistent and courageous fight" is the complete domination of democracy by the plutocracy.

For some inexplicable reason Ickes thinks that this time victory is assured, provided the people understand that the fight is "not between the New Deal and the average enlightened businessman, but between the New Deal and the Bourbons of the sixty families who have brought the rest of the businessmen in the United States under the terror of their domination." This authoritative spokesman does not explain just how the "Bourbons" managed to subjugate all the enlightened businessmen, notwithstanding democracy and the efforts of the "greatest historical figures." The Rockefellers, the Morgans, the Mellons, the Vanderbilts, the Guggenheims, the Fords & Co. did not invade the United States from the outside, as Cortez invaded Mexico : they grew organically out of the "people," or more precisely, out of the class of "enlightened industrialists and businessmen" and became, in line with Marx's prognosis, the natural apogee of capitalism. Since a young and strong democracy in its hey-day was unable to check the concentration of wealth when the process was only at its inception, is it possible to believe even for a minute that a decaying democracy is capable of weakening class antagonisms that have attained their utmost limit ? Anyway, the experience of the New Deal has produced no ground for such optimism. Refuting the charges of big business against the government, Robert H. Jackson, a person high in the councils of the administration, proved with figures that during Roosevelt's tenure the profits of the magnates of capital reached heights they themselves had ceased to dream about during the last period of Hoover's presidency, from which it follows, in any event, that Roosevelt's fight against monopolies has been crowned with no greater success than the struggle of all his predecessors.

TO BRING BACK YESTERDAY

One cannot but agree with Professor Lewis W. Douglas, the former Director of the Budget in the Roosevelt Administration, when he condemns the government for "attacking monopoly in one field while fostering monopoly in many others." Yet in the nature of the thing it cannot be otherwise. According to Marx, the government is the executive committee of the ruling class. Today monopolists are the strongest section of the ruling class. No government is in any position to fight against monopoly in general, i. e., against the class by whose will it rules. While attacking one phase of monopoly, it is obliged to seek an ally in other phases of monopoly. In union with banks and light industry it can deliver occasional blows against the trusts of heavy industry, which, by the way, do not stop earning fantastic profits because of that.

Lewis Douglas does not counterpose science to the official quackery, but merely another kind of quackery. He sees the source of monopoly not in capitalism but in protectionism and, accordingly, discovers the salvation of society not in the abolition of private ownership of the means of production but in the lowering of customs tariffs. "Unless the freedom of markets is restored," he predicts, it is "doubtful that the freedom of all institutions — enterprise, speech, education, religion — can survive." In other words, without restoring the freedom of international trade, democracy, wherever and to the extent that it has yet survived, must yield either to a revolutionary or to a fascist dictatorship. But freedom of international trade is inconceivable without freedom of internal trade, i. e., without competition. And freedom of competition is inconceivable under the sway of monopoly. Unfortunately, Mr. Douglas, quite like Mr. Ickes, like Mr. Jackson, like Mr. Cummings, and like Mr. Roosevelt himself, has not gone to the trouble to initiate us into his own prescription against monopolistic capitalism and thereby — against either a revolution or a totalitarian regime.

Freedom of trade, like freedom of competition, like the prosperity of the middle class, belongs to the irrevocable past. To bring back yesterday, is now the sole prescription of the democratic reformers of capitalism : to bring back more "freedom" to small and middle-sized industrialists and businessmen, to change the money and credit system in their favor, to free the market from being bossed by the trusts, to eliminate professional speculators from the stock exchange, to restore freedom of international trade, and so forth *ad infinitum*. The reformers even dream of limiting the use of machines and placing a proscription on technique, which disturbs the social balance and causes a lot of worry.

SCIENTISTS AND MARXISM

Speaking in defense of science on December 7, 1937, Dr. Robert A. Millikan, a leading American physicist, observed : "United States statistics show that the percentage of the population 'gainfully employed' has steadily increased during the last fifty years, when science has been most rapidly applied." This defense of capitalism under the guise of defending science cannot be called a happy one. It is precisely during the last half century that "was broken the link of times" and the interrelation of economics and technique altered sharply.

The period referred to by Millikan included the beginning of capitalist decline as well as the highest point of capitalist prosperity. To hush up the beginning of that decline, which is world-wide, is to stand forth as an apologist for capitalism. Rejecting Socialism in an offhand manner with the aid of arguments that would scarcely do honor even to Henry Ford, Dr. Millikan tells us that no system of distribution can satisfy the needs of man without raising the range of production. Undoubtedly! But it is a pity that the famous physicist did not explain to the millions of American unemployed just how they were to participate in raising the national income. Abstract preachment about the saving grace of individual initiative and high productivity of labor will certainly not provide the unemployed with jobs, nor will it fill the budgetary deficit, nor lead the nation's business out of its blind alley.

What distinguishes Marx is the universality of his genius, his ability to understand phenomena and processes of various fields in their inherent connection. Without being a specialist in natural sciences, he was one of the first to appreciate the significance of the great discoveries in that field ; for example, the theory of Darwinism. Marx was assured of that pre-eminence not so much by virtue of his intellect as by virtue of his method. Bourgeois-minded scientists may think that they are above Socialism ; yet Robert Millikan's case is but one more confirmation that in the sphere of sociology they continue to be hopeless quacks.

PRODUCTIVE POSSIBILITIES AND PRIVATE OWNERSHIP

In his message to Congress at the beginning of 1937 President Roosevelt expressed his desire to raise the national income to ninety or one hundred billion dollars, without however indicating just how. In itself this program is exceedingly modest. In 1929, when there were approximately two million unemployed, the national income reached eighty-one billion dollars. Setting in motion the present productive forces would not only suffice to realize Roosevelt's program but even to surpass it considerably. Machines, raw materials, workers, everything is available, not to mention the population's need for the products. If, notwithstanding that, the plan is unrealizable — and unrealizable it is — the only reason is the irreconcilable conflict that has developed between capitalist ownership and society's need for expanding production. The famous government-sponsored National Survey of Potential Productive Capacity came to the conclusion that the cost of production and services used in 1929 amounted to nearly ninety-four billion dollars, calculated on the basis of retail prices. Yet if all the actual productive possibilities were utilized, that figure would have risen to 135 billion dollars, which would have averaged $4370 a year per family, sufficient to secure a decent and comfortable living. It must be added that the calculations of the National Survey are based on the present productive organization of the United States, as it came about in consequence of capitalism's anarchic history. If the equipment itself were re-equipped on the basis of a unified socialist plan, the productive calculations could be considerably surpassed and a high comfortable standard of living, on the basis of an extremely short labor day, assured to all the people.

Therefore, to save society, it is not necessary either to check the development of technique, to shut down factories, to award premiums to farmers for sabotaging agriculture, to turn a third of the workers into paupers, or to call upon maniacs to be dictators. Not one of these measures, which are a shocking mockery of the interests of society, is necessary. What is indispensable and urgent is to separate the means of production from their present parasitic owners and to organize society in accordance with a rational plan. Then it would at once be possible really to cure society of its ills. All those able to work would find a job. The work day would gradually decrease. The wants of all members of society would secure increasing satisfaction. The words "poverty," "crisis," "exploitation," would drop out of circulation. Mankind would at last cross the threshold into true humanity.

THE INEVITABILITY OF SOCIALISM

"Along with the constantly diminishing number of the magnates of capital . . ." says Marx, "grows the mass of misery, oppression, slavery, degradation, exploitation ; but with this too grows the revolt of the working-class, a class always increasing in numbers, and disciplined, united, organized by the very mechanism of the process of capitalist production itself. . . Centralization of the means of production and socialization of labor at last reach a point where they become incompatible with their capitalist integument. This integument is burst asunder. The knell of capitalist private property sounds. The expropriators are expropriated." That is the Socialist revolution. To Marx, the problem of reconstituting society did not arise from some prescription, motivated by his personal predilections ; it followed, as an iron-clad historical necessity — on the one hand, from the productive forces grown to powerful maturity ; on the other, from the impossibility further to foster these forces at the mercy of the law of value.

The lucubrations of certain intellectuals on the theme that, regardless of Marx's teaching, socialism is not *inevitable* but merely *possible,* are devoid of any content whatsoever. Obviously, Marx did not imply that socialism would come about without man's volition and action : any such idea is simply an absurdity. Marx foretold that out of the economic collapse in which the development of capitalism must inevitably culminate — and this collapse is before our very eyes — there can be no other way out except socialization of the means of production. The productive forces need a new organizer and a new master, and, since existence determines consciousness, Marx had no doubt that the working class, at the cost of errors and defeats, will come to understand the actual situation and, sooner or later, will draw the imperative practical conclusions.

That socialization of the capitalist-created means of production is of tremendous economic benefit is today demonstrable not only in theory but also by the experiment of the U.S.S.R., notwithstanding the limitations of that experiment. True, capitalistic reactionaries, not without artifice, use Stalin's regime as a scarecrow against the ideas of socialism. As a matter of fact, Marx never said that socialism could be achieved in a single country, and moreover, a backward country. The continuing privations of the masses in the U.S.S.R., the omnipotence of the privileged caste, which has lifted itself above the nation and its misery, finally, the rampant club-law of the bureaucrats are not consequences of the socialist method of economy but of the isolation and backwardness of the U.S.S.R. caught in the ring of capitalist encirclement. The wonder is that under such exceptionally unfavorable conditions planned economy has managed to demonstrate its insuperable benefits.

All the saviors of capitalism, the democratic as well as the fascist kind, attempt to limit, or at least to camouflage, the power of the magnates of capital, in order to forestall "the expropriation of the expropriators." They all recognize, and many of them openly admit, that the failure of their reformist attempts must inevitably lead to socialist revolution. They have all managed to demonstrate that their methods of saving capitalism are but reactionary and helpless quackery. Marx's prognosis about the inevitability of socialism is thus fully confirmed by proof of the negative.

THE INEVITABILITY OF SOCIALIST REVOLUTION

The program of "Technocracy," which flourished in the period of the great crisis of 1929-1932, was founded on the correct premise that economy can be rationalized only through the union of technique at the height of science and government at the service of society. Such a union is possible, provided technique and government are liberated from the slavery of private ownership. That is where the great revolutionary task begins. In order to liberate technique from the cabal of private interests and place the government at the service of society, it is necessary to "expropriate the expropriators." Only a powerful class, interested in its own liberation and opposed to the monopolistic expropriators, is capable of consummating this task. Only in unison with a proletarian government can the qualified stratum of technicians build a truly scientific and a truly national, i. e., a socialist economy.

It would be best, of course, to achieve this purpose in a peaceful, gradual, democratic way. But the social order that has outlived itself never yields its place to its successor without resistance. If in its day the young forceful democracy proved incapable of forestalling the seizure of wealth and power by the plutocracy, is it possible to expect that a senile and devastated democracy will prove capable of transforming a social order based on the untrammelled rule of sixty families? Theory and history teach that a succession of social regimes presupposes the highest form of the class struggle, i. e., revolution. Even slavery could not be abolished in the United States without a civil war. "Force is the midwife of every old society pregnant with a new one." No one has yet been able to refute Marx on this basic tenet in the sociology of class society. Only a socialist revolution can clear the road to socialism.

MARXISM IN THE UNITED STATES

The North American republic has gone further than others in the sphere of technique and the organization of production. Not only Americans but all of mankind will build on that foundation. However, the various phases of the social process in one and the same nation have varying rhythms, depending on special historical conditions. While the United States enjoys tremendous superiority in technology, its economic thought is extremely backward in both the right and left wings. John L. Lewis has about the same views as Franklin D. Roosevelt. Considering the nature of his office, Lewis' social function is incomparably more conservative, not to say reactionary, than Roosevelt's. In certain American circles there is a tendency to repudiate this or that radical theory without the slightest scientific criticism, by simply dismissing it as "un-American." But where can you find the differentiating criterion of that? Christianity was imported into the United States along with logarithms, Shakespeare's poetry, notions on the rights of man and the citizen, and certain other not unimportant products of human thought. Today Marxism stands in the same category.

The American Secretary of Agriculture Henry A. Wallace imputed to the author of these lines ". . . a dogmatic thinness which is bitterly un-American" and counterposed to Russian dogmatism the opportunist spirit of Jefferson, who knew how to get along with his opponents. Apparently, it has never occurred to Mr. Wallace that a policy of compromise is not a function of some immaterial national spirit, but a product of material conditions. A nation rapidly growing rich has sufficient reserves for conciliation between hostile classes and parties. When, on the other hand, social contradictions are sharpened, the ground for compromise disappears. America was free of "dogmatic thinness" only because it had a plethora of virgin areas, inexhaustible resources of natural wealth and, it would seem, limitless opportunities for enrichment. True, even under these conditions the spirit of compromise did not prevent the Civil War when the hour for it struck. Anyway, the material conditions which made up the basis of "Americanism" are today increasingly relegated to the past. Hence the profound crisis of traditional American ideology.

Empiric thinking, limited to the solution of immediate tasks from time to time, seemed adequate enough in labor as well as in bourgeois circles as long as Marx's law of value did everybody's thinking. But today that very law produces opposite effects. Instead of urging economy forward, it undermines its foundations. Conciliatory eclectic thinking, maintaining an unfavorable or disdainful attitude towards Marxism as a "dogma," and with its philosophic apogee, pragmatism, becomes utterly inadequate, increasingly insubstantial, reactionary and downright funny.

On the contrary, it is the traditional ideas of "Americanism" that have become lifeless, petrified "dogma," giving rise to nothing but errors and confusion. At the same time, the economic teaching of Marx has acquired peculiar viability and pointedness for the United States. Although *Capital* rests on international material, preponderantly English, in its theoretical foundation it is an analysis of pure capitalism, capitalism in general, capitalism as such. Undoubtedly, the capitalism grown on the virgin, unhistorical soil of America comes closest to that ideal type of capitalism.

Saving Mr. Wallace's presence, America developed economically not in accordance with the principles of Jefferson, but in accordance with the laws of Marx. There is as little offense to national self-esteem in acknowledging this as in recognizing that America turns around the sun in accordance with the laws of Newton. *Capital* offers a faultless diagnosis of the malady and an irreplaceable prognosis. In that sense the teaching of Marx is far more permeated with new "Americanism" than the ideas of Hoover and Roosevelt, of Green and Lewis.

True, there is a widespread original literature in the United States devoted to the crisis of American economy. In so far as conscientious economists offer an objective picture of the destructive trends of American capitalism, their investigations, regardless of their theoretical premises, look like direct illustrations of Marx's theory. The conservative tradition makes itself known, however, when these authors stubbornly restrain themselves from definitive conclusions, limiting themselves to gloomy predictions or such edifying banalities as "the country must understand," "public opinion must earnestly consider," and the like. These books look like a knife without a blade.

The United States had Marxists in the past, it is true, but they were a strange type of Marxist, or rather, three strange types. In the first place, there were the émigrés cast out of Europe, who did what they could but could not find any response ; in the second place, isolated American groups, like the De Leonists, who in the course of events, and because of their own mistakes, turned themselves into sects ; in the third place, dilettantes attracted by the October Revolution and sympathetic to Marxism as an exotic teaching that had little to do with the United States. Their day is over. Now dawns the new epoch of an independent class movement of the proletariat and at the same time of – genuine Marxism. In this, too, America will in a few jumps catch up with Europe and outdistance it. Progressive technique and a progressive social structure will pave their own way in the sphere of doctrine. The best theoreticians of Marxism will appear on American soil. Marx will become the mentor of the advanced American workers. To them this abridged exposition of the first volume will become only an initial step towards the complete Marx.

CAPITALISM'S IDEAL MIRROR

At the time the first volume of *Capital* was published world domination by the British bourgeoisie was as yet unchallenged. The abstract laws of commodity economy naturally found their fullest embodiment – i. e., the one least dependent on past influences — in the country where capitalism had achieved its highest development. While relying in his analysis mainly on England, Marx had not only England in view, but the entire capitalist world. He used the England of his day as capitalism's best contemporaneous mirror.

Now only memories are left of British hegemony. The advantages of capitalistic primogeniture have turned into disadvántages. England's technical and economic structure has become outworn. The country continues to depend for its world position on the colonial empire, a heritage of the past, rather than on an active economic potential. That explains, incidentally, Chamberlain's Christian charity towards the international gangsterism of the fascists, which has so astonished everybody. The English bourgeoisie cannot help realizing that its economic decline has become thoroughly incompatible with its position in the world and that a new war threatens to bring about the downfall of the British Empire. Essentially similar is the economic basis of France's "pacificism."

Germany, on the contrary, has utilized in its rapid capitalistic ascent the advantages of historic backwardness, by arming itself with the most complete technique in Europe. Having a narrow national base and paucity of natural resources, Germany's dynamic capitalism of necessity became transformed into the most explosive factor in the so-called balance of world powers. Hitler's epileptic ideology is only a reflected image of the epilepsy of German capitalism.

In addition to numerous invaluable advantages of a historical character, the development of the United States enjoyed the pre-eminence of an immeasurably larger territory and incomparably greater natural wealth than Germany's. Having considerably outstripped Great Britain, the North American republic became at the beginning of this century the chief stronghold of the world bourgeoisie. There all the potentialities implanted in capitalism found their highest possible expression. Nowhere else on our planet can the bourgeoisie in any way exceed its achievements in the dollar republic, which has become for the twentieth century capitalism's most perfect mirror.

For the same reasons that Marx preferred to base his exposition on English statistics, English parliamentary reports, English "Blue Books," and the like, we have resorted in our modest introduction to evidence chiefly from the economic and political experience of the United States. It would not be difficult, needless to say, to cite analogous facts and figures from the life of any other capitalist country. But that would not add anything essential. The conclusions would remain the same, only the examples would be less striking.

The economic policy of the Popular Front in France was, as one of its financiers aptly put it, an adaptation of the New Deal "for Lilliputians." It is perfectly obvious that in a theoretical analysis it is immeasurably more convenient to deal with Cyclopean than with Lilliputian magnitudes. It is the very immensity of Roosevelt's experiment which shows that only a miracle can save the world-wide capitalist system. But it so happens that the development of capitalist production put a stop to the production of miracles. Incantations and prayers abound, miracles never come. However, it is clear that if the miracle of capitalism's rejuvenation could happen anywhere at all, it would be nowhere else but in the United States. Yet this rejuvenation was not achieved. What the Cyclops failed to attain the Lilliputians are even less able to accomplish. To lay the foundation for that simple conclusion, is the sense of our excursion into the field of American economy.

MOTHER COUNTRIES AND COLONIES

"The country that is more developed industrially," Marx wrote in the preface to the first edition of his *Capital*, "only shows to the less developed the image of its own future." Under no circumstances can this thought be taken literally. The growth of productive forces and the deepening of social inconsistencies is undoubtedly the lot of every country that has set out on the road of bourgeois development. However, the disproportion of tempos and standards, which goes through all of mankind's development, not only became especially acute under capitalism, but gave rise to the complex interdependence of subordination, exploitation, and oppression between countries of different economic type.

Only a minority of countries has fully gone through that systematic and logical development from handicraft through domestic manufacture to the factory, which Marx subjected to such detailed analysis. Commercial, industrial, and financial capital invaded backward countries from the outside, partly destroying the primitive forms of native economy and partly subjecting them to the world-wide industrial and banking system of the West. Under the whip of imperialism the colonies and semi-colonies found themselves compelled to disregard the intervening stages, at the same time artificially hanging on at one level or another. India's development did not duplicate England's development ; it was a supplement to it. However, in order to understand the combined type of development of backward and dependent countries like India, it is always necessary to bear in mind the classical schema Marx derived from England's development. The labor theory of value guides equally the calculations of speculators in London's City and the money changing transactions in the most remote corners of Haidarabad, except that in the latter case it assumes more simple and less crafty forms.

Disproportion of development brought tremendous benefits to the advanced countries, which, although in varying degrees, continued to develop at the expense of the backward ones, by exploiting them, by converting them into their colonies, or, at least, by making it im-

possible for them to get in among the capitalist aristocracy. The fortunes of Spain, Holland, England, France
were obtained not only from the surplus labor of their
own proletariat, not only by devastating their own *petit-
bourgeoisie*, but also through the systematic pillage of
their overseas possessions. The exploitation of classes
was supplemented, and its potency increased by the exploitation of nations.

The bourgeoisie of the mother countries was enabled
to secure a privileged position for its own proletariat,
especially the upper layers, by paying for it with some
of the super-profits garnered in the colonies. Without
that, any sort of stable democratic regime would have
been utterly impossible. In its expanded manifestation
bourgeois democracy became, and continues to remain,
a form of government accessible only to the most aris-
tocratic and the most exploitative nations. Ancient democracy was based on slavery, imperialist democracy
on the spoliation of colonies.

The United States, which formally has almost no
colonies, is nevertheless the most privileged of all the
nations of history. Active immigrants from Europe
took possession of an exceedingly rich continent, ex-
terminated the native population, seized the best part
of Mexico and bagged the lion's share of the world's
wealth. The deposits of fat thus accumulated continue
to be useful even now, in the epoch of decline, for
greasing the gears and wheels of democracy.

Recent historical experience, as well as theoretical
analysis, attests that the rate of a democracy's development and its stability are in inverse ratio to the tension
of class contradictions. In the less privileged capitalist
countries (Russia, on the one hand; Germany, Italy,
and the like, on the other), which were unable to en-
gender a numerous and stable labor aristocracy, democracy was never developed to any extent and succumbed
to dictatorship with comparative ease. However, the
continuing progressive paralysis of capitalism is prepar-

ing the same fate for the democracies of the most privileged and the richest nations : the only difference is in dates. The uncontrollable deterioration in the living conditions of the workers makes it less and less possible for the bourgeoisie to grant the masses the right of participation in political life, even within the limited framework of bourgeois parliamentarism. Any other explanation of the manifest process of democracy's dislodgment by fascism is an idealistic falsification of things as they are, either deception or self-deception.

While destroying democracy in the old mother countries of capital, imperialism at the same time hinders the rise of democracy in the backward countries. The fact that in the new epoch not a single one of the colonies or semi-colonies has consummated its democratic revolution — above all, in the field of agrarian relations — is entirely due to imperialism, which has become the chief brake on economic and political progress. Plundering the natural wealth of the backward countries and deliberately restraining their independent industrial development, the monopolistic magnates and their governments simultaneously grant financial, political, and military support to the most reactionary, parasitic, semi-feudal groups of native exploiters. Artificially preserved agrarian barbarism is today the most sinister plague of contemporary world economy. The fight of the colonial peoples for their liberation, passing over the intervening stages, transforms itself of necessity into a fight against imperialism, and thus aligns itself with the struggle of the proletariat in the mother countries. Colonial uprisings and wars in their turn rock the foundations of the capitalist world more than ever and render the miracle of its regeneration less than ever possible.

PLANNED WORLD ECONOMY

Capitalism achieved the twin historical merit of having placed technique on a high level and having bound all parts of the world with economic ties. Thus it pledged the material pre-requisites for the systematic utilization of all of our planet's resources. However, capitalism is in no position to fulfill this urgent task. The nidus of its expansion continues to consist of circumscribed nationalist states with their customs houses and armies. Yet the productive forces have long ago outgrown the boundaries of the national state, thereby transforming what was once a progressive historical factor into an unendurable restraint. Imperialist wars are nothing else than the detonations of productive forces against the state borders, which have come to be too confining for them. The program of so-called autarchy has nothing to do with going back to a self-sufficient circumscribed economy. It only means that the national base is being made ready for a new war.

After the Versailles Treaty was signed it was generally believed that the terrestrial globe had been pretty well subdivided. But more recent events have served to remind us that our planet continues to contain lands that have not yet been either plundered or sufficiently plundered. The struggle for colonies continues to be part and parcel of the policy of imperialistic capitalism. No matter how thoroughly the world is divided, the process never ends, but only again and again places on the order of the day the question of a new redivision of the world in line with altered relations between imperialistic forces. Such is the actual reason today for rearmaments, diplomatic convulsions, and war alignments.

All attempts to represent the impending war as a clash between the ideas of democracy and fascism belong to the realm either of charlatanism or stupidity. Political forms change, capitalist appetites remain. If a fascist regime were to be established tomorrow on either side of the English Channel — and hardly anyone will dare to deny such a possibility — the Paris and London dictators would be just as little able to give up their colonial possessions as Mussolini and Hitler their colonial claims. The furious and hopeless struggle for a new division of the world follows irresistibly from the mortal crisis of the capitalist system.

Partial reforms and patchwork will do no good. Historical development has come to one of those decisive stages when only the direct intervention of the masses is able to sweep away the reactionary obstructions and lay the foundations of a new regime. Abolition of private ownership in the means of production is the first pre-requisite to planned economy, i. e., the introduction of reason into the sphere of human relations, first on a national and eventually on a world scale. Once it begins, the socialist revolution will spread from country to country with immeasurably greater force than fascism spreads today. By the example and with the aid of the advanced nations, the backward nations will also be carried away into the main stream of socialism. The thoroughly rotted customs toll-gates will fall. The contradictions which rend Europe and the entire world asunder will find their natural and peaceful solution within the framework of a Socialist United States in Europe as well as in other parts of the world. Liberated humanity will draw itself up to its full height.

Leon Trotsky has had selected and arranged
the essence of Marx's thought from

CAPITAL : A CRITIQUE OF POLITICAL ECONOMY

CAPITAL

A CRITIQUE OF POLITICAL ECONOMY

THE PROCESS OF CAPITALIST PRODUCTION

I. COMMODITIES AND MONEY

1. *Commodities and Money*

The wealth of those societies in which the capitalist mode of production prevails, presents itself as "an immense accumulation of commodities," its unit being a single commodity. Our investigation must therefore begin with the analysis of a commodity.

A commodity is, in the first place, an object outside us, a thing that by its properties satisfies human wants of some sort or another. The nature of such wants, whether, for instance, they spring from the stomach or from fancy, makes no difference.

Every useful thing may be looked at from the two points of view of quality and quantity. It is an assemblage of many properties, and may therefore be of use in various ways. To discover the various use of things is the work of history.

The utility of a thing makes it a use-value. But this utility is not a thing of air. Being limited by the physical properties of the commodity, it has no existence apart from that commodity. A commodity, such as iron, corn, or a diamond, is therefore, so far as it is a material thing, a use-value, something useful.

Use-values become a reality only by use or consumption : they also constitute the substance of all wealth, whatever may be the social form of that wealth. They are, in addition, the material depositories of exchange value. Exchange value, at first sight, presents itself as a quantitative relation, as the proportion in which values in use of one sort are exchanged for those of another sort, a relation constantly changing with time and place.

Let us take two commodities, *e. g.*, corn and iron. The proportions in which they are exchangeable, whatever those proportions may be, can always be represented by an equation in which a given quantity of corn is equated to some quantity of iron. What does this equation tell us ? It tells us that in two different things there exists in equal quantities something common to both. The two things must therefore be equal to a third, which in itself is neither the one nor the other. Each of them, so far as it is exchange value, must therefore be reducible to this third.

This common "something" cannot be either a geometrical, a chemical, or any other natural property of commodities. Such properties claim our attention only in so far as they affect the utility of those commodities, make them use-values. But the exchange of commodities is evidently an act characterised by a total abstraction from use-value.

If then we leave out of consideration the use-value of commodities, they have only one common property left, that of being products of labour. But even the product of labour itself has undergone a change in our hands. We see in it no longer a table, a house, yarn, or any other useful thing. Its existence as a material thing is put out of sight. Neither can it any longer be regarded as the product of the labour of the joiner, the mason, the spinner, or of any other definite kind of productive labour. Along with the useful qualities of the products themselves, we put out of sight both the useful character of the various kinds of labour embodied in them, and the concrete forms of that labour ; there is nothing left but what is common to them all ; all are reduced to one and the same sort of labour, human labour in the abstract.

It consists of the same unsubstantial reality in each, a

mere congelation of homogeneous human labour, of labour-power expended without regard to the mode of its expenditure. When looked at as crystals of this social substance, common to them all, they are — Values.

A use-value, or useful article, therefore, has value only because human labour in the abstract has been embodied or materialised in it. How, then, is the magnitude of this value to be measured ? Plainly, by the quantity of the value-creating substance, the labour, contained in the article. The quantity of labour, however, is measured by its duration, and labour-time in its turn finds its standard in weeks, days, and hours.

The total labour-power of society, which is embodied in the sum total of the values of all commodities produced by that society, counts here as one homogeneous mass of human labour-power, composed though it be of innumerable individual units. Each of these units is the same as any other, so far as it has the character of the average labour-power of society, and takes effect as such ; that is, so far as it requires for producing a commodity, no more time than is needed on an average, no more than is socially necessary. The labour-time socially necessary is that required to produce an article under the normal conditions of production, and with the average degree of skill and intensity prevalent at the time. The introduction of power looms into England probably reduced by one half the labour required to weave a given quantity of yarn into cloth. The hand-loom weavers, as a matter of fact, continued to require the same time as before ; but for all that, the product of one hour of their labour represented after the change only half an hour's social labour, and consequently fell to one half its former value. We see then that that which determines the magnitude of the value of any article is the amount of labour socially necessary, or the labour-time socially necessary for its production. Each individual commodity, in this connexion, is to be considered as an average sample of its class.

The value of one commodity is to the value of any other, as the labour-time necessary for the production of the one is to that necessary for the production of the other. In general, the greater the productiveness of labour, the less is the labour-time required for the production of an article, the less is the amount of labour crystallised in that article, and the less is its value; and *vice versa*, the less the productiveness of labour, the greater is the labour-time required for the production of an article, and the greater is its value. The value of a commodity, therefore, varies directly as the quantity, and inversely as the productiveness, of the labour incorporated in it.

A thing can be a use-value, without having value. This is the case whenever its utility to man is not due to labour. Such are air, virgin soil, natural meadows, &c. A thing can be useful, and the product of human labour, without being a commodity. Whoever directly satisfies his wants with the produce of his own labour, creates, indeed, use-values, but not commodities. In order to produce the latter, he must not only produce use-values, but use-values for others, social use-values. Lastly, nothing can have value, without being an object of utility. If the thing is useless, so is the labour contained in it; the labour does not count as labour, and therefore creates no value.

Let us take two commodities such as a coat and 10 yards of linen, and let the former be double the value of the latter, so that, if 10 yards of linen = W, the coat = 2W.

The coat is a use-value that satisfies a particular want. Its existence is the result of a special sort of productive activity, the nature of which is determined by its aim, mode of operation, subject, means, and result. The labour, whose utility is thus represented by the value in use of its product, or which manifests itself by making its product a use-value, we call useful labour. In this connexion we consider only its useful effect.

As the coat and the linen are two qualitatively different use-values, so also are the two forms of labour that produce them, tailoring and weaving. To all the different varieties of values in use there correspond as many different kinds of useful labour, classified according to the order, genus, species, and variety to which they belong in the social division of labour. This division of labour is a necessary condition for the production of commodities, but it does not follow conversely, that the production of commodities is a necessary condition for the division of labour.

In a community, the produce of which in general takes the form of commodities, *i. e.*, in a community of commodity producers, this qualitative difference between the useful forms of labour that are carried on independently by individual producers, each on their own account, develops into a complex system, a social division of labour.

The use-values, coat, linen, &c., *i. e.*, the bodies of commodities, are combinations of two elements — matter and labour. Man can work only as Nature does, that is by changing the form of matter. Nay more, in this work of changing the form he is constantly helped by natural forces. We see, then, that labour is not the only source of material wealth, of use-values produced by labour. As William Petty puts it, labour is its father and the earth its mother.

Let us now pass from the commodity considered as a use-value to the value of commodities. By our assumption, the coat is worth twice as much as the linen. But this is a mere quantitative difference, which for the present does not concern us. We bear in mind, however, that if the value of the coat is double that of 10 yds. of linen, 20 yds. of linen must have the same value as one coat. So far as they are values, the coat and the linen are things of a like substance, objective expressions of essentially identical labour. But tailoring and weaving are, qualitatively, different kinds of labour. They are, however, each a productive expenditure of human brains, nerves, and muscles, and in this sense are human labour. They are but two different modes of expending human labour-power. But the value of a commodity represents human labour in the abstract, the expenditure of human labour in general.

Simple average labour, it is true, varies in character in different countries and at different times, but in a particular society it is given. Skilled labour counts only as simple labour intensified, or rather, as multiplied simple labour, a given quantity of skilled being considered equal to a greater quantity of simple labour.

Just as, therefore, in viewing the coat and linen as values, we abstract from their different use-values, so it is with the labour represented by those values : we disregard the difference between its useful forms, weaving and tailoring. As the use-values, coat and linen, are combinations of special productive activities with cloth and yarn, while the values, coat and linen, are, on the other hand, mere homogeneous congelations of undifferentiated labour, so the labour embodied in these latter values does not count by virtue of its productive relation to cloth and yarn, but only as being expenditure of human labour-power.

Coats and linen, however, are not merely values, but values of definite magnitude, and according to our assumption, the coat is worth twice as much as the ten yards of linen. Whence this difference in their values ? It is owing to the fact that the linen contains only half as much labour as the coat, and consequently, that in the production of the latter, labour-power must have been expended during twice the time necessary for the production of the former.

An increase in the quantity of use-values is an increase of material wealth. With two coats two men can be clothed, with one coat only one man. Nevertheless, an increased quantity of material wealth may correspond to a simultaneous fall in the magnitude of its value.

This antagonistic movement has its origin in the two-fold character of labour. On the one hand all labour is, speaking physiologically, an expenditure of human labour-power, and in its character of identical abstract human labour, it creates and forms the value of commodities. On the other hand, all labour is the expenditure of human labour-power in a special form and with a definite aim, and in this, its character of concrete useful labour, it produces use-values.

I was the first to point out and to examine critically this twofold nature of the labour contained in commodities. As this point is the pivot on which a clear comprehension of political economy turns, we must go more into detail.

Commodities come into the world in the shape of use-values, articles, or goods. This is their plain, homely, bodily form. They are, however, commodities, only because they are something twofold, both objects of utility, and, at the same time, depositories of value. They manifest themselves therefore as commodities, or have the form of commodities, only in so far as they have two forms, a physical or natural form, and a value form.

If we say that, as values, commodities are mere congelations of human labour, we reduce them by our analysis, it is true, to the abstraction, value ; but we ascribe to this value no form apart from their bodily form. It is otherwise in the value relation of one commodity to another. Here, the one stands forth in its character of value by reason of its relation to the other.

The simplest value relation is evidently that of one commodity to some one other commodity of a different kind. Hence the relation between the values of two commodities supplies us with the simplest expression of the value of a single commodity.

The whole mystery of the form of value lies hidden in this elementary form. Its analysis, therefore, is our real difficulty. Here two different kinds of commodities (in our example the linen and the coat), evidently play two different parts. The linen expresses its value in the coat ; the coat serves as the material in which that value is expressed. The former plays an active, the latter a passive, part. The value of the linen is represented as relative value, or appears in relative form. The coat officiates as equivalent, or appears in equivalent form.

The relative form and the equivalent form are two intimately connected, mutually dependent and inseparable elements of the expression of value ; but, at the same time, are mutually exclusive, antagonistic extremes — i. e., poles of the same expression. They are allotted respectively to the two different commodities brought into relation by that expression.

Whether, then, a commodity assumes the relative form, or the opposite equivalent form, depends entirely upon its accidental position in the expression of value — that is, upon whether it is the commodity whose value is being expressed or the commodity in which value is being expressed.

When occupying the position of equivalent in the equation of value, the coat ranks qualitatively as the equal of the linen, as something of the same kind, because it is value. In this position it is a thing in which we see nothing but value, or whose palpable bodily form represents value. In the production of the coat, human labour-power, in the shape of tailoring, must have been actually expended. Human labour is therefore accumulated in it. In this aspect the coat is a depository of value, but though worn to a thread, it does not let this fact show through. And as equivalent of the linen in the value equation, it exists under this aspect alone, counts therefore as embodied value, as a body that is value.

Hence, in the value equation in which the coat is the equivalent of the linen, the coat officiates as the form of value. The value of the commodity linen is expressed by the bodily form of the commodity coat, the value of one by the use-value of the other.

All that our analysis of the value of commodities has already told us, is told us by the linen itself, so soon as it comes into communication with another commodity, the coat. Only it betrays its thoughts in that language with which alone it is familiar, the language of commodities. In order to tell us that its own value is created by labour in its abstract character of human labour, it says that the coat, in so far as it is worth as much as the linen, and therefore is value, consists of the same labour as the linen. In order to inform us that its sublime reality as value is not the same as. its buckram body, it says that value has the appearance of a coat, and consequently that so far as the linen is value, it and the coat are as like as two peas.

The equation, 20 yards of linen = 1 coat, or 20 yards of linen are worth one coat, implies that the same quantity of value-substance (congealed labour) is embodied in both ; that the two commodities have each cost the same amount of labour or the same quantity of labour time. But the labour time necessary for the production of 20 yards of linen or 1 coat varies with every change in the productiveness of weaving or tailoring. We have now to consider the influence of such changes on the quantitative aspect of the relative expression of value :

I. The value of the linen may vary, that of the coat remaining constant. II. The value of the linen may remain constant, while the value of the coat varies. III. The quantities of labour time respectively necessary for the production of the linen and the coat may vary simultaneously in the same direction and in the same proportion. IV. The labour time respectively necessary for the production of the linen and the coat, and therefore the value of these commodities may simultaneously vary in the same direction, but at unequal rates, or in opposite directions, or in other ways. The relative value of a commodity may vary, although its value remains constant. Its relative value may remain constant, although its value varies; finally, simultaneous variations in the magnitude of value and in that of its relative expression by no means necessarily correspond in amount.

When we say that a commodity is in the equivalent form, we express the fact that it is directly exchangeable with other commodities.

The first peculiarity that strikes us, in considering the form of the equivalent, is this : use-value becomes the form of manifestation, the phenomenal form of its opposite, value. The bodily form of the commodity becomes its value form. The second peculiarity of the equivalent form is, that concrete labour becomes the form under which its opposite, abstract human labour, manifests itself.

The opposition or contrast existing internally in each commodity between use-value and value, is, therefore, made evident externally by two commodities being placed in such relation to each other, that the commodity whose value it is sought to express, figures directly as a mere use-value, while the commodity in which that value is to be expressed, figures directly as mere exchange value. Hence the elementary form of value of a commodity is the elementary form in which the contrast contained in that commodity, between use-value and value, becomes apparent.

Nevertheless, the elementary form of value passes by an easy transition into a more complete form. Therefore, according as it is placed in relation with one or the other, we get for one and the same commodity, different elementary expressions of value. The number of such possible expressions is limited only by the number of the different kinds of commodities distinct from it. The isolated expression of the value of a commodity is therefore convertible into a series, prolonged to any length, of the different elementary expressions of that value.

The linen, by virtue of the form of its value, now stands in a social relation, no longer with only one other kind of commodity, but with the whole world of commodities. As a commodity, it is a citizen of that world. At the same time, the interminable series of value equations implies, that as regards the value of a commodity, it is a matter of indifference under what particular form, or kind, of use-value it appears.

In the first form, 20 yds. of linen = 1 coat, it might for ought that otherwise appears be pure accident, that these two commodities are exchangeable in definite quantities. In the second form, on the contrary, we perceive at once the background that determines, and is essentially different from, this accidental appearance.

But in the first place, the relative expression of value is incomplete because the series representing it is interminable. In the second place, it is a many-coloured mosaic of disparate and independent expressions of value. And lastly, if, as must be the case, the relative value of each commodity in turn, becomes expressed in this expanded form, we get for each of them a relative-value form, different in every case, and consisting of an interminable series of expressions of value.

The defects of the expanded relative-value form are reflected in the corresponding equivalent form. The accidental relation between two individual commodity-owners disappears. It becomes plain, that it is not the exchange of commodities which regulates the magnitude of their value ; but, on the contrary, that it is the magnitude of their value which controls their exchange proportions.

When a person exchanges his linen for many other

commodities, and thus expresses its value in a series of
other commodities, it necessarily follows, that the various owners of the latter exchange them for the linen,
and consequently express the value of their various commodities in one and the same third commodity, the linen.
We get a general form of value : 1 coat = 20 yards of
linen, 10 lbs. of tea = 20 yards of linen, 40 lbs. of coffee
= 20 yards of linen, 1 quarter of corn = 20 yards of
linen, 2 ounces of gold = 20 yards of linen, ½ a ton of
iron = 20 yards of linen, x com. A, = 20 yards of
linen, etc. All commodities now express their value (1)
in an elementary form, because in a single commodity ;
(2) with unity, because in one and the same commodity.

The value of every commodity is now, by being
equated to linen, not only differentiated from its own
use-value, but from all other use-values generally, and
is, by that very fact, expressed as that which is common
to all commodities. By this form, commodities are,
for the first time, effectively brought into relation with
one another as values, or made to appear as exchange
values.

The general value form, which represents all products
of labour as mere congelations of undifferentiated human labour, shows by its very structure that it is the
social resumé of the world of commodities. That form
consequently makes it indisputably evident that in the
world of commodities the character possessed by all
labour of being *human* labour constitutes its specific
social character.

The degree of development of the relative form of
value corresponds to that of the equivalent form. But
we must bear in mind that the development of the latter
is only the expression and result of the development of
the former. The primary relative form of value of one
commodity converts some other commodity into an
isolated equivalent. The expanded form of relative
value, which is the expression of the value of one com-

modity in terms of all other commodities, endows those other commodities with the character of particular equivalents differing in kind. And lastly, a particular kind of commodity acquires the character of universal equivalent, because all other commodities make it the material in which they uniformly express their value.

A single commodity, the linen, appears therefore to have acquired the character of direct exchangeability with every other commodity because, and in so far as, this character is denied to every other commodity. The commodity that figures as universal equivalent, is, on the other hand, excluded from the relative-value form.

The particular commodity, with whose bodily form the equivalent form is thus socially identified, now becomes the money commodity, or serves as money. It becomes the special social function of that commodity, and consequently its social monopoly, to play within the world of commodities the part of the universal equivalent.

This foremost place has been attained by one in particular — namely, gold.

We get the money form: 20 yards of linen = 2 ounces of gold, 1 coat = 2 ounces of gold, 10 ℔ of tea = 2 ounces of gold, 40 ℔ of coffee = 2 ounces of gold, 1 qr. of corn = 2 ounces of gold, ½ a ton of iron = 2 ounces of gold, x commodity A = 2 ounces of gold.

Gold is now money with reference to all other commodities only because it was previously, with reference to them, a simple commodity. Like all other commodities, it was also capable of serving as an equivalent, either as simple equivalent in isolated exchanges, or as particular equivalent by the side of others. Gradually it began to serve, within varying limits, as universal equivalent.

So soon as it monopolises this position in the expression of value for the world of commodities, it becomes the money commodity, and then, and not till then, does the general form of value become changed into the money form.

A commodity appears, at first sight, a very trivial thing, and easily understood. Its analysis shows that it is, in reality, a very queer thing, abounding in metaphysical subtleties and theological niceties. So far as it is a value in use, there is nothing mysterious about it. It is as clear as noon-day, that man, by his industry, changes the forms of the materials furnished by nature, in such a way as to make them useful to him. The form of wood, for instance, is altered, by making a table out of it. Yet, for all that the table continues to be that common, every-day thing, wood.

But, so soon as it steps forth as a commodity, it is changed into something transcendent. It not only stands with its feet on the ground, but, in relation to all other commodities, it stands on its head, and evolves out of its wooden brain grotesque ideas, far more wonderful than "table-turning" ever was.

The mystical character of commodities does not originate in their use-value. Just as little does it proceed from the nature of the determining factors of value. Whence, then, arises the enigmatical character of the product of labour, so soon as it assumes the form of commodities ? Clearly from this form itself.

A commodity is therefore a mysterious thing, simply because in it the social character of men's labour appears to them as an objective character stamped upon the product of that labour ; because the relation of the producers to the sum total of their own labour is presented to them as a social relation, existing not between themselves, but between the products of their labour. This is the reason why the products of labour become commodities, social things whose qualities are at the same time perceptible and imperceptible by the senses. There it is a definite social relation between men, that assumes, in their eyes, the fantastic form of a relation between things. In order, therefore, to find an analogy, we must have recourse to the mist-enveloped regions of the religious world. In that world the productions of the human brain appear as independent beings endowed with life, and entering into relation both with one another and the human race. So it is in the world of commodities with the products of men's hands. This I call the Fetishism which attaches itself to the products of labour, so soon as they are produced as commodities, and which is therefore inseparable from the production of commodities.

This Fetishism of commodities has its origin in the peculiar social character of the labour that produces them. As a general rule, articles of utility become commodities, only because they are products of the labour of private individuals or groups of individuals who carry on their work independently of each other. The sum total of the labour of all these private individuals forms the aggregate labour of society. Since the producers do not come into social contact with each other until they exchange their products, the specific social character of each producer's labour does not show itself except in the act of exchange. In other words, the labour of the individual asserts itself as a part of the labour of society, only by means of the relations which the act of exchange establishes directly between the products, and indirectly, through them, between the producers. To the latter, therefore, the relations connecting the labour of one individual with that of the rest appear, not as direct social relations between individuals at work, but as what they really are, material relations between persons and social relations between things.

It is only by being exchanged that the products of labour acquire, as values, one uniform social status, distinct from their varied forms of existence as objects of utility. From this moment the labour of the individual producer acquires socially a twofold character. On the

one hand, it must, as a definite useful kind of labour,
satisfy a definite social want, and thus hold its place as
part and parcel of the collective labour of all, as a branch
of a social division of labour that has sprung up spontaneously. On the other hand, it can satisfy the manifold wants of the individual producer himself, only in
so far as the mutual exchangeability of all kinds of useful private labour is an established social fact, and therefore the private useful labour of each producer ranks
on an equality with that of all others.

The twofold social character of the labour of the individual appears to him, when reflected in his brain, only
under those forms which are impressed upon that labour
in everyday practice by the exchange of products. In
this way, the character that his own labour possesses of
being socially useful takes the form of the condition,
that the product must be not only useful, but useful for
others, and the social character that his particular labour
has of being the equal of all other particular kinds of
labour, takes the form that all the physically different
articles that are the products of labour, have one common quality, viz., that of having value.

Hence, when we bring the products of our labour
into relation with each other as values, it is not because
we see in these articles the material receptacles of homogeneous human labour. Quite the contrary ; whenever, by an exchange, we equate as values our different
products, by that very act, we also equate, as human
labour, the different kinds of labour expended upon
them. We are not aware of this, nevertheless we do it.
Value, therefore, does not stalk about with a label describing what it is. It is value, rather, that converts
every product into a social hieroglyphic. Later on, we
try to decipher the hieroglyphic, to get behind the secret of our own social products ; for to stamp an object
of utility as a value, is just as much a social product as
language. The recent scientific discovery, that the prod--
ucts of labour, so far as they are values, are but material

expressions of the human labour spent in their production, marks, indeed, an epoch in the history of the development of the human race, but, by no means, dissipates the mist through which the social character of labour appears to us to be an objective character of the products themselves.

When I state that coats or boots stand in a relation to linen, because it is the universal incarnation of abstract human labour, the absurdity of the statement is self-evident. Nevertheless, when the producers of coats and boots compare those articles with linen, or, what is the same thing with gold or silver, as the universal equivalent, they express the relation between their own private labour and the collective labour of society in the same absurd form. The categories of bourgeois economy consist of such like forms. They are forms of thought expressing with social validity the conditions and relations of a definite, historically determined mode of production, viz., the production of commodities. The whole mystery of commodities, all the magic and necromancy that surrounds the products of labour as long as they take the form of commodities, vanishes therefore, so soon as we come to other forms of production.

Could commodities themselves speak, they would say : Our use-value may be a thing that interests men. It is no part of us as objects. What, however, does belong to us as objects, is our value. Our natural intercourse as commodities proves it. In the eyes of each other we are nothing but exchange values. It is a peculiar circumstance that the use-value of objects is realised without exchange, by means of a direct relation between the objects and man, while, on the other hand, their value is realised only by exchange, that is, by means of a social process. Who fails here to call to mind our good friend, Dogberry, who informs neighbour Seacoal, that, "To be a well-favoured man is the gift of fortune ; but reading and writing comes by nature" ?

2. *Exchange*

It is plain that commodities cannot go to market and make exchanges of their own account. We must, therefore, have recourse to their guardians, who are also their owners. Commodities are things, and therefore without power of resistance against man. If they are wanting in docility he can use force ; in other words, he can take possession of them. In order that these objects may enter into relation with each other as commodities, their guardians must place themselves in relation to one another, as persons whose will resides in those objects, and must behave in such a way that each does not appropriate the commodity of the other, and part with his own, except by means of an act done by mutual consent. They must, therefore, mutually recognise in each other the right of private proprietors.

This juridical relation, which thus expresses itself in a contract, whether such contract be part of a developed legal system or not, is a relation between two wills, and is but the reflex of the real economical relation between the two. It is this economical relation that determines the subject matter comprised in each such juridical act. The persons exist for one another merely as representatives of, and, therefore, as owners of, commodities. The characters who appear on the economic stage are but the personifications of the economical relations that exist between them.

His commodity possesses for the owner no immediate use-value. Otherwise, he would not bring it to the market. It has use-value for others ; for himself its only direct use-value is that of being a depository of exchange value, and consequently, a means of exchange. Therefore, he makes up his mind to part with it for commodities whose value in use is of service to him. All commodities are non-use-values for their owners, and use-values for their non-owners.

Consequently, they must all change hands. But this

change of hands is what constitutes their exchange, and the latter puts them in relation with each other as values, and realises them as values. Hence commodities must be realised as values before they can be realised as use-values. On the other hand, they must show that they are use-values before they can be realised as values. For the labour spent upon them counts effectively, only in so far as it is spent in a form that is useful for others. Whether that labour is useful for others and its product consequently capable of satisfying the wants of others, can be proved only by the act of exchange.

Every owner of a commodity wishes to part with it in exchange only for those commodities whose use-value satisfies some want of his. Looked at in this way, exchange is for him simply a private transaction. On the other hand, he desires to realise the value of his commodity, to convert it into any other suitable commodity of equal value. From this point of view, exchange is for him a social transaction of a general character. But one and the same set of transactions cannot be simultaneously for all owners of commodities both exclusively private and exclusively social and general.

The exchange of commodities, therefore, first begins on the boundaries of such communities, at their points of contact with other similar communities, or with members of the latter. So soon, however, as products once become commodities in the external relations of a community, they also, by reaction, become so in its internal intercourse. The proportions in which they are exchangeable are at first quite a matter of chance. Meantime the need for foreign objects of utility gradually establishes itself. The constant repetition of exchange makes it a normal social act. In the course of time, therefore, some portion at least of the products of labour must be produced with a special view to exchange. From that moment the distinction becomes firmly established between the utility of an object for the purposes of consumption, and its utility for the purposes of exchange. Its use-value becomes distinguished from its exchange value. On the other hand, the quantitative proportion in which the articles are exchangeable, becomes dependent on their production itself. Custom stamps them as values with definite magnitudes.

In the direct barter of products, each commodity is directly a means of exchange to its owner, and to all other persons an equivalent, but that only in so far as it has use-value for them. At this stage, therefore, the articles exchanged do not acquire a value-form independent of their own use-value. The necessity for a value-form grows with the increasing number and variety of the commodities exchanged. The problem and the means of solution arise simultaneously.

A special article, by becoming the equivalent of various other commodities, acquires at once, though within narrow limits, the character of a general social equivalent. This character comes and goes with the momentary social acts that called it into life. In turns and transiently it attaches itself first to this and then to that commodity. The particular kind of commodity to which it sticks is at first a matter of accident. Nevertheless there are two circumstances whose influence is decisive. The money-form attaches itself either to the most important articles of exchange from outside, or else it attaches itself to the object of utility that forms, like cattle, the chief portion of indigenous alienable wealth. Man has often made man himself, under the form of slaves, serve as the primitive material of money, but has never used land for that purpose. Such an idea could only spring up in a bourgeois society already well developed.

Money is a crystal formed of necessity in the course of the exchanges, whereby different products of labour are practically equated to one another and thus by practice converted into commodities. At the same rate, then, as the conversion of products into commodities is being accomplished, so also is the conversion of one special commodity into money.

An adequate form of manifestation of value, a fit embodiment of abstract, undifferentiated, and therefore equal human labour, that material alone can be whose every sample exhibits the same uniform qualities. On the other hand, since the difference between the magnitudes of value is purely quantitative, the money commodity must be susceptible of merely quantitative differences, must therefore be divisible at will, and equally capable of being re-united. Gold and silver possess these properties by nature.

The money-form is but the reflex, thrown upon one single commodity, of the value relations between all the rest. That money is a commodity is therefore a new discovery only for those who, when they analyse it, start from its fully developed shape. The act of exchange gives to the commodity converted into money, not its value, but its specific value-form. By confounding these two distinct things some writers have been led to hold that the value of gold and silver is imaginary. The fact that money can, in certain functions, be replaced by mere symbols of itself, gave rise to that other mistaken notion, that it is itself a mere symbol.

Money, like every other commodity, cannot express the magnitude of its value except relatively in other commodities. This value is determined by the labour-time required for its production, and is expressed by the quantity of any other commodity that costs the same amount of labour-time. When it steps into circulation as money, its value is already given.

What appears to happen is, not that gold becomes money, in consequence of all other commodities expressing their values in it, but, on the contrary, that all other commodities universally express their values in gold, because it is money. The intermediate steps of the process vanish in the result and leave no trace behind.

Commodities find their own value already completely represented, without any initiative on their part, in another commodity existing in company with them. These objects, gold and silver, just as they come out of the bowels of the earth, are forthwith the direct incarnation of all human labour. Hence the magic of money.

The riddle presented by money is but the riddle presented by commodities; only it now strikes us in its most glaring form.

3. *Money, or the Circulation of Commodities*

The first chief function of money is to supply commodities with the material for the expression of their values, or to represent their values as magnitudes of the same denomination, qualitatively equal, and quantitatively comparable. It thus serves as a *universal measure of value*. And only by virtue of this function does gold, the equivalent commodity *par excellence*, become money.

It is not money that renders commodities commensurable. Just the contrary. It is because all commodities, as values, are realised human labour, and therefore commensurable, that their values can be measured by one and the same special commodity, and the latter be converted into the common measure of their values, *i.e.*, into money. Money, as a measure of value, is the phenomenal form that must of necessity be assumed by that measure of value which is immanent in commodities, labour-time.

The expression of the value of a commodity in gold is its money-form or price.

The price of commodities is, like their form of value generally, a form quite distinct from their palpable bodily form; it is, therefore, a purely ideal or mental form. Their owner must, therefore, lend them his tongue, or hang a ticket on them, before their prices can be communicated to the outside world. Every trader knows that it does not require the least bit of real gold to estimate in that metal millions of pounds' worth of goods.

If gold and silver are simultaneously measures of value, all commodities have two prices — one a gold-price, the other a silver-price. These exist quietly side by side, so long as the ratio of the value of silver to that of gold remains unchanged.

The values of commodities are changed in imagination into so many different quantities of gold. Hence, in spite of the confusing variety of the commodities themselves, their values become magnitudes of the same denomination, gold-magnitudes. They are now capable of being compared with each other and measured, and the want becomes technically felt of comparing them with some fixed quantity of gold as a unit measure. This unit, by subsequent division into aliquot parts, becomes itself the standard or scale. Before they become money, gold, silver, and copper already possess such standard measures in their standards of weight.

As *measure of value* and as *standard of price*, money has two entirely distinct functions to perform. It is the measure of value inasmuch as it is the socially recognised incarnation of human labour ; it is the standard of price inasmuch as it is a fixed weight of metal. As the measure of value it serves to convert the values of all the manifold commodities into prices, into imaginary quantities of gold ; as the standard of price it measures those quantities of gold. The measure of values measures commodities considered as values ; the standard of price measures, on the contrary, quantities of gold by a unit quantity of gold, not the value of one quantity of gold by the weight of another. In order to make gold a standard of price, a certain weight must be fixed upon as the unit. The less the unit is subject to variation, so much the better does the standard of price fulfill its office.

No matter how this value varies, the proportions between the values of different quantities of the metal remain constant.

A general rise in the prices of commodities can result only, either from a rise in their values — the value of money remaining constant — or from a fall in the value of money, the values of commodities remaining constant. On the other hand, a general fall in prices can result only, either from a fall in the values of commodities — the value of money remaining constant — or from a rise in the value of money, the values of commodities remaining constant. It therefore by no means follows, that a rise in the value of money necessarily implies a proportional fall in the prices of commodities ; or that a fall in the value of money implies a proportional rise in prices. Such change of price holds good only in the case of commodities whose value remains constant.

By degrees there arises a discrepancy between the current money names of the various weights of the precious metal figuring as money, and the actual weights which those names originally represented. The word pound, for instance, was the money-name given to an actual pound weight of silver. When gold replaced silver as a measure of value, the same name was applied according to the ratio between the values of silver and gold, to perhaps one fifteenth of a pound of gold. The word pound, as a money-name, thus becomes differentiated from the same word as a weight-name.

Since the standard of money is on the one hand purely conventional, and must on the other hand find general acceptance, it is in the end regulated by law. A given weight of one of the precious metals, an ounce of gold, for instance, becomes officially divided into aliquot parts, with legally bestowed names, such as pound, dollar, &c. These aliquot parts, which henceforth serve as units of money, are then subdivided into other aliquot parts with legal names, such as shilling, penny, &c. But, both before and after these divisions are made, a definite weight of metal is the standard of metallic money. The sole alteration consists in the subdivision and denomination.

In this way commodities express by their prices how much they are worth, and money serves as *money of account* whenever it is a question of fixing the value of an article in its money-form.

Price is the money-name of the labour realised in a commodity. Hence the expression of the equivalence of a commodity with the sum of money constituting its price, is a tautology, just as in general the expression of the relative value of a commodity is a statement of the equivalence of two commodities.

But although price, being the exponent of the magnitude of a commodity's value, is the exponent of its exchange-ratio with money, it does not follow that the exponent of this exchange-ratio is necessarily the exponent of the magnitude of the commodity's value.

Magnitude of value expresses a relation of social production, it expresses the connection that necessarily exists between a certain article and the portion of the total labour-time of society required to produce it. As soon as magnitude of value is converted into price, the above necessary relation takes the shape of a more or less accidental exchange-ratio between a single commodity and another, the money-commodity. But this exchange-ratio may express either the real magnitude of that commodity's value, or the quantity of gold deviating from that value, for which, according to circumstances, it may be parted with.

The possibility, therefore, of quantitative incongruity between price and magnitude of value is inherent in the price-form itself. This is no defect, but, on the contrary, admirably adapts the price-form to a mode of production whose inherent laws impose themselves only as the mean of apparently lawless irregularities that compensate one another.

The price-form may conceal a qualitative inconsistency, so much so, that, although money is nothing but the value-form of commodities, price ceases altogether to express value. Objects that in themselves are no commodities, such as conscience, honour, &c., are capable of being offered for sale by their holders, and of thus acquiring, through their price, the form of commodities. Hence an object may have a price without having value. The price in that case is imaginary, like certain quantities in mathematics. On the other hand, the imaginary price-form may sometimes conceal either a direct or indirect real value-relation ; for instance, the price of uncultivated land, which is without value, because no human labour has been incorporated in it.

A price therefore implies both that a commodity is exchangeable for money, and also that it must be so exchanged. On the other hand, gold serves as an ideal measure of value, only because it has already, in the process of exchange, established itself as the money-commodity. Under the ideal measure of values there lurks the hard cash.

In so far as exchange is a process, by which commodities are transferred from hands in which they are non-use-values, to hands in which they become use-values, it is a social circulation of matter. The product of one form of useful labour replaces that of another. When once a commodity has found a resting-place, where it can serve as a use-value, it falls out of the sphere of exchange into that of consumption. But the former sphere alone interests us at present. We have, therefore, now to consider exchange from a formal point of view ; to investigate the change of form or metamorphosis of commodities which effectuates the social circulation of matter.

The comprehension of this change of form is, as a rule, very imperfect. The cause of this imperfection is, apart from indistinct notions of value itself, that every change of form in a commodity results from the exchange of two commodities, an ordinary one and the money-commodity. If we keep in view the material fact alone we overlook the very thing that we ought to observe — namely, what has happened to the form of the commodity. We overlook the facts that gold, when a mere commodity, is not money, and that when other commodities express their prices in gold, this gold is but the money-form of those commodities themselves.

Commodities, first of all, enter into the process of exchange just as they are. The process then differentiates them into commodities and money, and thus produces an external opposition corresponding to the internal opposition inherent in them, as being at once use-values and values. Commodities as use-values now stand opposed to money as exchange value. On the other hand, both opposing sides are commodities, unities of use-value and value. But this unity of differences manifests itself at two opposite poles, and at each pole in an opposite way. Being poles they are as necessarily opposite as they are connected. On the one side of the equation we have an ordinary commodity, which is in reality a use-value. Its value is expressed only ideally in its price, by which it is equated to its opponent, the gold, as to the real embodiment of its value. On the other hand, the gold, in its metallic reality ranks as the embodiment of value, as money. Gold, as gold, is exchange value itself. These antagonistic forms of commodities are the real forms in which the process of their exchange moves and takes place.

The exchange becomes an accomplished fact by two metamorphoses of opposite yet supplementary character, and by the following changes in their form :

Commodity (C) — Money (M) — Commodity (C)

But the apparently single process is in reality a double one. From the pole of the commodity owner it is a sale, from the opposite pole of the money owner, it is

a purchase. In other words, a sale is a purchase, C — M
is also M — C. As the person who makes a sale, the
owner is a seller ; as the person who makes a purchase,
he is a buyer.

The complete metamorphosis of a commodity, in its
simplest form, implies four extremes, and three drama-
tis personæ. First, a commodity comes face to face with
money ; the latter is the form taken by the value of
the former, and exists in all its hard reality, in the pocket
of the buyer. A commodity-owner is thus brought into
contact with a possessor of money. So soon, now, as the
commodity has been changed into money, the money
becomes its transient equivalent-form, the use-value of
which equivalent-form is to be found in the bodies of
other commodities. Money, the final term of the first
transmutation, is at the same time the starting point for
the second. The person who is a seller in the first transaction thus becomes a buyer in the second, in which a
third commodity-owner appears on the scene as a seller.

The two phases, each inverse to the other, that make
up the metamorphosis of a commodity constitute together a circular movement, a circuit : commodity-
form, stripping off of this form, and return to the
commodity-form. No doubt, the commodity appears
here under two different aspects. At the starting point
it is not a use-value to its owner ; at the finishing point
it is. So, too, the money appears in the first phase as a
solid crystal of value, a crystal into which the commodity eagerly solidifies, and in the second, dissolves into
the mere transient equivalent-form destined to be replaced by a use-value.

The circuit made by one commodity in the course
of its metamorphoses is inextricably mixed up with the
circuits of other commodities. The total of all the different circuits constitutes *the circulation of commodities.*

Nothing can be more childish than the dogma, that
because every sale is a purchase, and every purchase a

sale, therefore the circulation of commodities necessarily implies an equilibrium of sales and purchases. Sale and purchase constitute one identical act, an exchange between a commodity-owner and an owner of money, between two persons as opposed to each other as the two poles of a magnet. The identity implies that the commodity is useless, if, on being thrown into the alchemistical retort of circulation, it does not come out again in the shape of money ; implies that the exchange, if it does take place, constitutes a period of rest, an interval, long or short, in the life of the commodity. No one can sell unless some one else purchases. But no one is forthwith bound to purchase, because he has just sold. Circulation bursts through all restrictions as to time, place, and individuals, imposed by direct barter, and this it effects by splitting up, into the antithesis of a sale and a purchase, the direct identity. To say that these two independent and antithetical acts have an intrinsic unity, are essentially one, is the same as to say that this intrinsic oneness expresses itself in an external antithesis. If the interval in time between the two complementary phases of the complete metamorphosis of a commodity becomes too great, if the split between the sale and the purchase becomes too pronounced, their oneness asserts itself by producing — a crisis.

The movement of the commodity is a circuit. On the other hand, the form of this movement precludes a circuit from being made by the money. The result is not the return of the money, but its continued removal further and further away from its starting-point.

In the first phase of its circulation the commodity changes place with the money. Thereupon the commodity, under its aspect of a useful object, falls out of circulation into consumption. In its stead we have its value-shape — the money. It then goes through the second phase of its circulation, not under its own natural shape, but under the shape of money.

The continuity of the movement is therefore kept up

by the money alone, and the same movement that as regards the commodity consists of two processes of an antithetical character, is, when considered as the movement of the money, always one and the same process, a continued change of places with ever fresh commodities. Hence the result brought about by the circulation of commodities, namely, the replacing of one commodity by another, takes the appearance of having been effected not by means of the change of form of the commodities, but rather by the money acting as a medium of circulation, by an action that circulates commodities, to all appearance motionless in themselves. Money is continually withdrawing commodities from circulation and stepping into their places, and in this way continually moving further and further from its starting-point.

Hence, although the movement of the money is merely the expression of the circulation of commodities, yet the contrary appears to be the actual fact, and the circulation of commodities seems to be the result of the movement of the money. Again, money functions as a means of circulation, only because in it the values of commodities have independent reality. Hence its movement, as the medium of circulation, is, in fact, merely the movement of commodities while changing their forms.

Money keeps continually within the sphere of circulation, and moves about in it. The question arises, how much money does this sphere absorb?

Since money and commodities always come bodily face to face, it is clear that the amount of the means of circulation required is determined beforehand by the sum of the prices of all these commodities. As a matter of fact, the money in reality represents the quantity or sum of gold ideally expressed beforehand by the sum of the prices of the commodities. The equality of these two sums is therefore self-evident.

We know, however, that, the values of commodities remaining constant, their prices vary with the value of gold, rising in proportion as it falls, and falling in proportion as it rises. Now if, in consequence of such a rise or fall in the value of gold, the sum of the prices of commodities fall or rise, the quantity of money in currency must fall or rise to the same extent. The change in the quantity of the circulating medium is, in this case, it is true, caused by money itself, yet not in virtue of its function as a medium of circulation, but of its function as a measure of value. First, the price of the commodities varies inversely as the value of the money, and then the quantity of the medium of circulation varies directly as the price of the commodities.

Exactly the same thing would happen if, for instance, instead of the value of gold falling, gold were replaced by silver as the measure of value, or if, instead of the value of silver rising, gold were to thrust silver out from being the measure of value. In each case the value of the material of money, *i.e.*, the value of the commodity that serves as the measure of value, would have undergone a change, and therefore, so, too, would the prices of commodities which express their values in money, and so, too, would the quantity of money current whose function it is to realise those prices.

If we consider the value of gold to be given, and if now we further suppose the price of each commodity to be given, the sum of the prices clearly depends on the mass of commodities in circulation. If the mass of commodities remain constant, the quantity of circulating money varies with the fluctuations in the prices of those commodities. It increases and diminishes because the sum of the prices increases or diminishes in consequence of the change of price.

The velocity of that currency reflects the rapidity with which commodities change their forms, the continued interlacing of one series of metamorphoses with another, the hurried social interchange of matter, the rapid disappearance of commodities from the sphere of circulation, and the equally rapid substitution of fresh ones in their places. On the other hand, the retardation of the currency reflects the separation of these two processes into isolated antithetical phases, reflects the stagnation in the change of form, and therefore, in the social interchange of matter.

The total quantity of money functioning during a given period as the circulating medium, is determined, on the one hand, by the sum of the prices of the circulating commodities, and on the other hand, by the rapidity with which the antithetical phases of the metamorphoses follow one another.

The three factors, however, state of prices, quantity of circulating commodities, and velocity of money-currency, are all variable. Hence, the sum of the prices to be realised, and consequently the quantity of the circulating medium depending on that sum, will vary with the numerous variations of these three factors in combination.

That money takes the shape of coin, springs from its function as the circulating medium. The weight of gold represented in imagination by the prices or money-names of commodities, must confront those commodities, within the circulation, in the shape of coins or pieces of gold of a given denomination. Coining, like the establishment of a standard of prices, is the business of the State.

During their currency, coins wear away, some more, others less. Name and substance, nominal weight and real weight, begin their process of separation. Coins of the same denomination become different in value, because they are different in weight.

This fact implies the latent possibility of replacing metallic coins by tokens of some other material, by symbols serving the same purposes as coins.

The tokens keep company with gold, to pay fractional parts of the smallest gold coin.

The weight of metal in the silver and copper tokens is arbitrarily fixed by law. When in currency, they wear away·even more rapidly than gold coins. Therefore things that are relatively without value, such as paper notes, can serve as coins in its place. We allude here only to inconvertible paper money issued by the State and having compulsory circulation.

Some one may ask why gold is capable of being replaced by tokens that have no value. But it is capable of being so replaced only in so far as it functions exclusively as coin, or as the circulating medium, and as nothing else. Each piece of money is a mere coin, or means of circulation, only so long as it actually circulates. The minimum mass of gold remains constantly within the sphere of circulation, continually functions as a circulating medium, and exists exclusively for that purpose. Its movement therefore represents nothing but the continued alternation of the inverse phases of the metamorphosis $C - M - C$, phases in which commodities confront their value-forms, only to disappear again immediately. The independent existence of the exchange value of a commodity is here a transient apparition, by means of which the commodity is immediately replaced by another commodity. Hence, in this process which continually makes money pass from hand to hand, the mere symbolical existence of money suffices. Its functional existence absorbs, so to say, its material existence. Being a transient and objective reflex of the prices of commodities, it serves only as a symbol of itself, and is therefore capable of being replaced by a token. One thing is, however, requisite ; this token must have an objective social validity of its own, and this the paper symbol acquires by its forced currency.

But as soon as the series of metamorphoses is interrupted, as soon as sales are not supplemented by subsequent purchases, money becomes petrified into a hoard. Hoarding serves various purposes in the economy of the metallic circulation. In order that the mass of money, actually current, may constantly saturate the absorbing power of the circulation, it is necessary that the quantity of gold and silver in a country be greater than the quantity required to function as coin. This condition is fulfilled by money taking the form of hoards. These reserves serve as conduits for the supply or withdrawal of money to or from the circulation, which in this way never overflows its banks.

The development of money into a medium of payment makes it necessary to accumulate money against the dates fixed for the payment of the sums owing. While hoarding, as a distinct mode of acquiring riches, vanishes with the progress of civil society, the formation of reserves of the means of payment grows with that progress.

Credit-money springs directly out of the function of money as a means of payment. Certificates of the debts owing for the purchased commodities circulate for the purpose of transferring those debts to others.

When the production of commodities has sufficiently extended itself, money begins to serve as the means of payment beyond the sphere of the circulation of commodities. It becomes the commodity that is the universal subject-matter of all contracts.

When money leaves the home sphere of circulation, it strips off the local garbs which it there assumes, of a standard of prices, of coin, of tokens, and of a symbol of value, and returns to its original form of bullion. In the trade between the markets of the world, the value of commodities is expressed so as to be universally recognised. Hence their independent value-form also, in these cases, confronts them under the shape of universal money. It is only in the markets of the world that money acquires to the full extent the character of the commodity whose bodily form is also the immediate social incarnation of human labour in the abstract.

II. The Transformation of Money into Capital

4. The Transformation of Money into Capital

The circulation of commodities is the starting point of capital. The production of commodities, their circulation, and that more developed form of their circulation called commerce, these form the historical groundwork from which it rises. The modern history of capital dates from the creation in the 16th century of a world-embracing commerce and a world-embracing market.

All new capital, to commence with, comes on the stage, that is, on the market, whether of commodities, labour, or money, even in our days, in the shape of money that by a definite process has to be transformed into capital.

The first distinction we notice between money that is money only, and money that is capital, is nothing more than a difference in their form of circulation. The simplest form of the circulation of commodities is C — M — C, the transformation of commodities into money, and the change of the money back again into commodities ; or selling in order to buy. But alongside of this form we find another specifically different form : M — C — M, the transformation of money into commodities, and the change of commodities back again into money ; or buying in order to sell. Money that circulates in the latter manner is thereby transformed into, becomes capital, and is already potentially capital.

In the first phase, M — C, or the purchase, the money is changed into a commodity. In the second phase, C — M, or the sale, the commodity is changed back again into money. The result, in which the phases of the process vanish, is the exchange of money for money, M — M.

The circuit M — C — M would be absurd and without

meaning if the intention were to exchange by this means two equal sums of money.

In the circulation $C - M - C$, the money is in the end converted into a commodity, that serves as a use-value ; it is spent once for all. The circuit $M - C - M$, on the contrary, commences with money and ends with money. Its leading motive, and the goal that attracts it, is therefore mere exchange value. One sum of money is distinguishable from another only by its amount. The character and tendency of the process $M - C - M$, is therefore not due to any qualitative difference between its extremes, but solely to their quantitative difference.

The exact form of this process is therefore $M - C - M'$, where $M' = M + \triangle M = $ the original sum advanced, plus an increment. This increment or excess over the original value I call "surplus-value." The value originally advanced, therefore, not only remains intact while in circulation, but adds to itself a surplus-value or expands itself. It is this movement that converts it into capital.

The simple circulation of commodities — selling in order to buy — is a means of carrying out a purpose unconnected with circulation, namely, the satisfaction of wants. The circulation of money as capital is, on the contrary, an end in itself, for the expansion of value takes place only within this constantly renewed movement. The circulation of capital has therefore no limits. Thus the conscious representative of this movement, the possessor of money becomes a capitalist. His person, or rather his pocket, is the point from which the money starts and to which it returns. The expansion of value, which is the objective basis or main-spring of the circulation, becomes his subjective aim. It functions as capital personified and endowed with consciousness and a will. The restless never-ending process of profit-making alone is what he aims at.

This boundless greed after riches, this passionate chase after exchange-value, is common to the capitalist and the miser ; but while the miser is merely a capitalist gone mad, the capitalist is a rational miser. The never-ending augmentation of exchange-value, which the miser strives after, by seeking to save his money from circulation, is attained by the more acute capitalist, by constantly throwing it afresh into circulation.

Value therefore now becomes value in process, money in process, and, as such, capital. It comes out of circulation, enters into it again, preserves and multiplies itself within its circuit, comes back out of it with expanded bulk, and begins the same round ever afresh. M — M', money which begets money, such is the description of Capital from the mouths of its first interpreters, the Mercantilists.

The change of value that occurs in the case of money intended to be converted into capital, cannot take place in the money itself, since in its function of means of purchase and of payment, it does no more than realise the price of the commodity it buys or pays for ; and, as hard cash, it is value petrified, never varying. Just as little can it originate in the re-sale of the commodity, which does no more than transform the article from its bodily form back again into its money-form. The change originates in the use-value of the commodity.

In order to be able to extract value from the consumption of a commodity, our friend, Moneybags, must be so lucky as to find, in the market, a commodity, whose use-value possesses the peculiar property of being a source of value, whose actual consumption, therefore, is itself an embodiment of labour, and, consequently, a creation of value.

The possessor of money does find on the market such a special commodity in capacity for labour or labour-power. By it is to be understood the aggregate of those

mental and physical capabilities existing in a human being, which he exercises whenever he produces a use-
value of any description.

He and the owner of money meet in the market, and
deal with each other as on the basis of equal rights, with
this difference alone, that one is buyer, the other seller ;
both, therefore, equal in the eyes of the law. The con-
tinuance of this relation demands that the owner of the
labour-power should sell it only for a definite period,
for if he were to sell it rump and stump, once for all,
he would be selling himself, converting himself from
a free man into a slave, from an owner of a commodity
into a commodity. He must constantly look upon his
labour-power as his own property, his own commodity,
and this he can only do by placing it at the disposal of
the buyer temporarily, for a definite period of time.
By this means alone can he avoid renouncing his rights
of ownership over it.

This peculiar commodity, labour-power, like all others, has a value. How is that value determined ? The
value of labour-power is determined, as in the case of
every other commodity, by the labour-time necessary
for the production, and consequently also the reproduction, of this special article. Labour-power exists only as
a capacity, or power of the living individual. Its production consequently presupposes his existence. Given
the individual, the production of labour-power consists
in his reproduction of himself or his maintenance. For
his maintenance he requires a given quantity of the
means of subsistence. Therefore the labour-time requisite for the production of labour-power reduces itself
to that necessary for the production of those means of
subsistence ; in other words, the value of labour-power
is the value of the means of subsistence necessary for the
maintenance of the labourer. His means of subsistence
must therefore be sufficient to maintain him in his normal state as a labouring individual.

His natural wants, such as food, clothing, fuel, and

housing, vary according to the climatic and other physical conditions of his country. On the other hand, the
number and extent of his so-called necessary wants, as
also the modes of satisfying them, are themselves the
product of historical development, and depend therefore to a great extent on the degree of civilisation of a
country. Nevertheless, in a given country, at a given
period, the average quantity of the means of subsistence
necessary for the labourer is practically known.

One consequence of the peculiar nature of labour-
power as a commodity is, that its use-value does not, on
the conclusion of this contract between the buyer and
seller, immediately pass into the hands of the former.
Its use-value consists in the subsequent exercise of its
force, in the consumption of the labour-power. In every country in which the capitalist mode of production
reigns, it is the custom not to pay for labour-power before it has been exercised for the period fixed by the
contract. In all cases, therefore, the use-value of the
labour-power is advanced to the capitalist; he everywhere gives credit to the capitalist.

The consumption of labour-power is at one and the
same time the production of commodities and of surplus value. The consumption of labour-power is com-
pleted, as in the case of every other commodity, outside
the limits of the market or of the sphere of circulation, within the hidden abode of production.

III. THE PRODUCTION OF ABSOLUTE SURPLUS-VALUE

5. The Labour-Process and the Process of Producing Surplus-Value

The capitalist buys labour-power in order to use it;
and labour-power in use is labour itself. The purchaser
of labour-power consumes it by setting the seller of it
to work.

Labour is, in the first place, a process in which both

man and Nature participate, and in which man of his own accord starts, regulates, and controls the material re-actions between himself and Nature.

We presuppose labour in a form that stamps it as exclusively human. A spider conducts operations that resemble those of a weaver, and a bee puts to shame many an architect in the construction of her cells. But what distinguishes the worst architect from the best of bees is this, that the architect raises his structure in imagination before he erects it in reality. At the end of every labour-process, we get a result that already existed in the imagination of the labourer at its commencement. He not only effects a change of form in the material on which he works, but he also realises a purpose of his own that gives the law to his *modus operandi*, and to which he must subordinate his will.

The elementary factors of the labour-process are 1, the personal activity of man, *i.e.*, work itself, 2, the subject of that work, and 3, its instruments.

All raw material is the subject of labour, but not every subject of labour is raw material; it can only become so, after it has undergone some alteration by means of labour. With the exception of the extractive industries, in which the material for labour is provided immediately by Nature, such as mining, hunting, fishing, and so on, all branches of industry manipulate raw material, objects already filtered through labour, already products of labour.

An instrument of labour is a thing, or a complex of things, which the labourer interposes between himself and the subject of his labour, and which serves as the conductor of his activity. He makes use of the mechanical, physical, and chemical properties of some substances in order to make other substances subservient to his aims. No sooner does labour undergo the least development, than it requires specially prepared instruments.

In the labour-process, therefore, man's activity, with

the help of the instruments of labour, effects an alteration, designed from the commencement, in the material worked upon. The process disappears in the product; the latter is a use-value. Labour has incorporated itself with its subject : the former is materialised, the latter transformed. The blacksmith forges and the product is a forging.

If we examine the whole process from the point of view of its result, the product, it is plain that both the instruments and the subject of labour, are means of production, and that the labour itself is productive labour.

Whether a use-value is to be regarded as raw material, as instrument of labour, or as product, this is determined entirely by its function in the labour process, by the position it there occupies.

The capitalist purchases, in the open market, all the necessary factors of the labour-process ; its objective factors, the means of production, as well as its subjective factor, labour-power. He then proceeds to consume the commodity, the labour-power that he has just bought, by causing the labourer, the impersonation of that labour-power, to consume the means of production by his labour.

The labour-process, the process by which the capitalist consumes labour-power, exhibits two characteristic phenomena : first, the labourer works under the control of the capitalist to whom his labour belongs ; secondly, the product is the property of the capitalist and not that of the labourer, its immediate producer. By the purchase of labour-power, the capitalist incorporates labour, as a living ferment, with the lifeless constituents of the product. From his point of view, the labour-process is nothing more than the consumption of the commodity purchased, i.e., of labour-power ; but this consumption cannot be effected except by supplying the labour-power with the means of production.

The aim of the capitalist is to produce not only a use-value, but a commodity also ; not only use-value, but value ; not only value, but at the same time surplus-value.

Just as commodities are, at the same time, use-values and values, so the process of producing them must be a labour-process, and at the same time, a process of creating value.

If the process of producing value be not carried beyond the point where the value paid by the capitalist for the labour-power is replaced by an exact equivalent, it is simply a process of producing value ; if it be continued beyond that point, it becomes a process of creating surplus-value.

The value of a day's labour-power amounts to 3 shillings, because the means of subsistence that are daily required for the production of labour-power, cost half a day's labour. The value of labour-power, and the value which that labour-power creates in the labour process, are two entirely different magnitudes ; and this difference of the two values was what the capitalist had in view, when he was purchasing the labour-power. The useful qualities that labour-power possesses, and by virtue of which it makes yarn or boots, were to him nothing more than a *conditio sine qua non* ; for in order to create value, labour must be expended in a useful manner. What really influenced him was the specific use-value which this commodity possesses of being *a source not only of value, but of more value than it has itself*. This is the special service that the capitalist expects from labour-power, and in this transaction he acts in accordance with the "eternal laws" of the exchange of commodities. The seller of labour-power, like the seller of any other commodity, realises its exchange-value, and parts with its use-value. He cannot take the one without giving the other. The use-value of labour-power, or in other words, labour, belongs just as little to its seller, as the use-value of oil after it has been sold belongs to the dealer who has sold it. The owner of the money has paid the value of a day's labour-power ; his, therefore, is the use of it for a day ; a day's labour belongs to him. The circumstance, that on the one hand the daily sustenance of labour-power costs only half a day's labour, while on the other hand the very same labour-power can work during a whole day, that consequently the value which its use during one day creates, is double what he pays for that use, this circumstance is, without doubt, a piece of good luck for the buyer, but by no means an injury to the seller.

The labourer therefore finds, in the workshop, the means of production necessary for working, not only during six, but during twelve hours. The capitalist, as buyer, paid for each commodity, for the cotton, the spindle and the labour-power, its full value. Equivalent was exchanged for equivalent. He then did what is done by every purchaser of commodities ; he consumed their use-value. The consumption of the labour-power, which was also the process of producing commodities, resulted in a product. The capitalist, formerly a buyer, now returns to market as a seller, of commodities. He withdraws 3 shillings more from circulation than he originally threw into it. This metamorphosis, this conversion of money into capital, takes place both within the sphere of circulation and also outside it ; within the circulation, because conditioned by the purchase of the labour-power in the market ; outside the circulation, because what is done within it is only a stepping-stone to the production of surplus-value, a process which is entirely confined to the sphere of production. By turning his money into commodities that serve as the material elements of a new product, and as factors in the labour-process, by incorporating living labour with their dead substance, the capitalist at the same time converts value, *i.e.*, past, materialised, and dead labour into capital, into value big with value.

Viewed as a value-creating process, the same labour-process presents itself under its quantitative aspect alone. Here it is a question merely of the time occupied by the labourer in doing the work ; of the period during which the labour-power is usefully expended. That labour, whether previously embodied in the means of production, or incorporated in them for the first time during the process by the action of labour-power, counts in either case only according to its duration.

Moreover, only so much of the time spent in the production of any article is counted, as, under the given social conditions, is necessary. The consequences of this are various. In the first place, it becomes necessary that the labour should be carried on under normal conditions. If a self-acting mule is the implement in general use for spinning, it would be absurd to supply the spinner with a distaff and spinning wheel. The cotton too must not be such rubbish as to cause extra waste in being worked, but must be of suitable quality. Whether the material factors of the process are of normal quality or not, depends entirely upon the capitalist. Then again, the labour-power itself must be of average efficacy. In the trade in which it is being employed, it must possess the average skill, handiness and quickness prevalent in that trade, and must be applied with the average amount of exertion and with the usual degree of intensity ; the capitalist is careful to see that this is done. He has bought the use of the labour-power for a definite period, and he insists upon his rights. He has no intention of being robbed. Lastly, all wasteful consumption of raw material or instruments of labour is strictly forbidden.

The process of production, considered on the one hand as the unity of the labour-process and the process of creating value, is production of commodities ; considered on the other hand as the unity of the labour-process and the process of producing surplus-value, it is the capitalist process of production, or capitalist production of commodities.

In the creation of surplus-value it does not in the least matter, whether the labour appropriated by the capitalist be simple unskilled labour of average quality or more complicated skilled labour. All labour of a higher or more complicated character than average labour is expenditure of labour-power of a more costly kind, labour-power whose production has cost more time and labour, and which therefore has a higher value, than unskilled or simple labour-power. Its consumption is labour of a higher class, labour that creates in equal times proportionally higher values than unskilled labour does. The surplus-value results only from a quantitative excess of labour, from a lengthening-out of one and the same labour-process.

6. *Constant Capital and Variable Capital*

The various factors of the labour-process play different parts in forming the value of the product. The labourer adds fresh value to the subject of his labour by expending upon it a given amount of additional labour. On the other hand, the values of the means of production used up in the process are preserved, and present themselves afresh as constituent parts of the value of the product. The value of the means of production is therefore preserved, by being transferred to the product. This transfer takes place during the conversion of those means into a product, or in other words, during the labour-process. It is brought about by labour ; but how ?

Since the addition of new value to the subject of his labour, and the preservation of its former value, are two entirely distinct results, produced simultaneously by the labourer, during one operation, it is plain that this twofold nature of the result can be explained only by the twofold nature of his labour ; at one and the same time, it must in one character create value, and in another character preserve or transfer value.

It is by virtue of its general character, as being expenditure of human labour-power in the abstract, that spinning adds new value to the values of the cotton and the spindle ; and on the other hand, it is by virtue of its special character, as being a concrete, useful process, that the same labour of spinning both transfers the values of the means of production to the product, and preserves them in the product. Hence at one and the same time there is produced a twofold result.

So long as the conditions of production remain the same, the more value the labourer adds by fresh labour, the more value he transfers and preserves ; but he does so merely because this addition of new value takes place under conditions that have not varied and are independent of his own labour. Of course, it may be said in one sense, that the labourer preserves old value always in proportion to the quantity of new value that he adds.

In the labour-process the means of production transfer their value to the product only so far as along with their use-value they lose also their exchange-value. They give up to the product that value alone which they themselves lose as means of production. The maximum loss of value that they can suffer in the process, is plainly limited by the amount of the original value with which they came into the process. Therefore the means of production can never add more value to the product than they themselves possess independently of the process in which they assist.

The same instrument of production takes part as a whole in the labour-process, while at the same time as an element in the formation of value, it enters only by fractions. On the other hand, a means of production may take part as a whole in the formation of value, while into the labour-process it enters only bit by bit.

In the value of the product, there is a re-appearance

of the value of the means of production, but there is, strictly speaking, no reproduction of that value. That which is produced is a new use-value in which the old exchange-value re-appears.

The surplus of the total value of the product, over the sum of the values of its constituent factors, is the surplus of the expanded capital over the capital originally advanced. The means of production on the one hand, labour-power on the other, are merely the different modes of existence which the value of the original capital assumed when from being money it was transformed into the various factors of the labour-process.

That part of capital which is represented by the means of production, by the raw material, auxiliary material and the instruments of labour, does not, in the process of production, undergo any quantitative alteration of value. I therefore call it the constant part of capital, or, more shortly, *constant capital*.

On the other hand, that part of capital, represented by labour-power, does, in the process of production, undergo an alteration of value. It both reproduces the equivalent of its own value, and also produces an excess, a surplus-value, which may itself vary, may be more or less according to circumstances. This part of capital is continually being transformed from a constant into a variable magnitude. I therefore call it the variable part of capital, or, shortly, *variable capital*.

The same elements of capital which, from the point of view of the labour-process, present themselves respectively as the objective and subjective factors, present themselves, from the point of view of the process of creating surplus-value, as constant and variable capital.

7. *The Rate of Surplus-Value*

The surplus-value generated in the process of production by C, the capital advanced, or in other words, the self-expansion of the value of the capital C, presents itself for our consideration, in the first place, as a surplus, as the amount by which the value of the product exceeds the value of its constituent element. We have seen that the labourer, during one portion of the labour-process, produces only the value of his labour-power, that is, the value of his means of subsistence. Now since his work forms part of a system, based on the social division of labour, he does not directly produce the actual necessaries which he himself consumes ; he produces instead a particular commodity, yarn for example, whose value is equal to the value of those necessaries or of the money with which they can be bought. The portion of his day's labour devoted to this purpose, will be greater or less, in proportion to the value of the necessaries that he daily requires on an average, or, what amounts to the same thing, in proportion to the labour-time required on an average to produce them. That portion of the working day, then, during which this reproduction takes place, I call "*necessary*" labour-time, and the labour expended during that time I call "*necessary*" labour. Necessary, as regards the labourer, because independent of the particular social form of his labour ; necessary, as regards capital, and the world of capitalists, because on the continued existence of the labourer depends their existence also.

During the second period of the labour-process, that in which his labour is no longer necessary labour, the workman, it is true, labours, expends labour-power ; but his labour, being no longer necessary labour, he creates no value for himself. He creates surplus-value which, for the capitalist, has all the charms of a creation out of nothing. This portion of the working day, I name surplus-labour-time, and to the labour expended during that time, I give the name of surplus-labour. It is every bit as important, for a correct understanding of surplus-value, to conceive it as a mere congelation of surplus-labour-time, as nothing but materialised surplus-labour, as it is, for a proper comprehension of value, to conceive it as a mere congelation of so many hours of labour, as nothing but materialised labour.

The essential difference between the various economic forms of society, between, for instance, a society based on slave labour, and one based on wage labour, lies only in the mode in which this surplus-labour is in each case extracted from the actual producer, the labourer.

Since, on the one hand, the value of this labour-power determines the necessary portion of the working day ; and since, on the other hand, the surplus-value is determined by the surplus portion of the working day, it follows that surplus-value bears the same ratio to variable capital, that surplus-labour does to necessary labour, or in other words, the rate of surplus-value $\frac{s}{v} = \frac{\text{surplus labor}}{\text{necessary labor}}$. Both ratios, $\frac{s}{v}$ and $\frac{\text{surplus labor}}{\text{necessary labor}}$ express the same thing in different ways ; in the one case by reference to materialised, incorporated labour, in the other by reference to living, fluent labour.

The rate of surplus-value is therefore an exact expression for the degree of exploitation of labour-power by capital, or of the labourer by the capitalist.

The method of calculating the rate of surplus-value is therefore, shortly, as follows. We take the total value of the product and put the constant capital which merely re-appears in it, equal to zero. What remains, is the only value that has, in the process of producing the commodity, been actually created. If the amount of surplus-value be given, we have only to deduct it from this remainder, to find the variable capital. And *vice versa*, if the latter be given, and we require to find the surplus-value. If both be given, we have only to perform the concluding operation, viz., to calculate $\frac{s}{v}$, the ratio of the surplus-value to the variable capital.

An example shows us how the capitalist converts money into capital. The product of a working day of

12 hours is 20 lbs. of yarn, having a value of 30s. No less than $\frac{8}{10}$ of this value, or 24s., is due to mere reappearance in it, of the value of the means of production (20 lbs. of cotton, value 20s., and spindle worn away, 4s.) : it is therefore constant capital. The remaining $\frac{2}{10}$ or 6s. is the new value created during the spinning process : of this one half replaces the value of the day's labour-power, or the variable capital, the remaining half constitutes a surplus-value of 3s. The total value then of the 20 lbs. of yarn is made up as follows : 30s. value of yarn = 24 const. + 3s. var. + 3s. surpl. Since the whole of the value is contained in the 20 lbs. of yarn produced, it follows that the various component parts of this value, can be represented as being contained respectively in corresponding parts of the product.

Since 12 working hours of the spinner are embodied in 6s., it follows that in yarn of the value of 30s., there must be embodied 60 working hours. And this quantity of labour-time does in fact exist in the 20 lbs. of yarn ; for in $\frac{8}{10}$ or 16 lbs. there are materialised the 48 hours of labour expended, before the commencement of the spinning process, on the means of production ; and in the remaining $\frac{2}{10}$ or 4 lbs. there are materialised the 12 hours' work done during the process itself.

On a former page we saw that the value of the yarn is equal to the sum of the new value created during the production of that yarn plus the value previously existing in the means of production. It has now been shown how the various component parts of the value of the product, parts that differ functionally from each other, may be represented by corresponding proportional parts of the product itself.

To split up in this manner the product into different parts, of which one represents only the labour previously spent on the means of production, or the constant capital, another, only the necessary labour spent during the process of production, or the variable capital, and another and last part, only the surplus-labour expended during the same process, or the surplus-value; to do this, is, as will be seen later on from its application to complicated and hitherto unsolved problems, no less important than it is simple.

The portion of the product that represents the surplus-value, we call "surplus-produce." Since the production of surplus-value is the chief end and aim of capitalist production, it is clear that the greatness of a man's or a nation's wealth should be measured, not by the absolute quantity produced, but by the relative magnitude of the surplus-produce.

8. *The Working Day*

The sum of the necessary labour and the surplus-labour, *i.e.*, of the periods of time during which the workman replaces the value of his labour-power, and produces the surplus-value, this sum constitutes the actual time during which he works, *i.e.*, the working day.

The working day is not a constant, but a variable quantity. One of its parts, certainly, is determined by the working time required for the reproduction of the labour-power of the labourer himself. But its total amount varies with the duration of the surplus-labor. The working day is, therefore, determinable, but is, *per se*, indeterminate.

The minimum limit is, however, not determinable. On the other hand, the working day has a maximum limit. It cannot be prolonged beyond a certain point. Within the 24 hours of the natural day a man can expend only a definite quantity of his vital force. During part of the day this force must rest, sleep; during another part the man has to satisfy other physical needs. Besides these purely physical limitations, the extension of the working day encounters moral ones. The labourer needs time for satisfying his intellectual and social wants, the extent and number of which are conditioned by the general state of social advancement. The variation of the working day fluctuates, therefore, within physical and social bounds. But both these limiting conditions are of a very elastic nature, and allow the greatest latitude.

The capitalist has bought the labour-power at its day-rate. To him its use-value belongs during one working day. He has thus acquired the right to make the labourer work for him during one day. But what is a working day?

The capitalist has his own views of the necessary limit of the working day. As capitalist, he is only capital personified. His soul is the soul of capital. But capital has one single life impulse, the tendency to create value and surplus-value, to make its constant factor, the means of production, absorb the greatest possible amount of surplus-labour. Capital is dead labour, that vampire-like, only lives by sucking living labour, and lives the more, the more labour it sucks. The time during which the labourer works, is the time during which the capitalist consumes the labour-power he has purchased of him. If the labourer consumes his disposable time for himself, he robs the capitalist. The capitalist then takes his stand on the law of the exchange of commodities. He, like all other buyers, seeks to get the greatest possible benefit out of the use-value of his commodity.

Suddenly the voice of the labourer rises : The commodity that I have sold to you differs from the crowd of other commodities, in that its use creates value, and a value greater than its own. That is why you bought it. That which on your side appears a spontaneous expansion of capital, is on mine extra expenditure of labour-power. You and I know on the market only one law, that of the exchange of commodities. And the consumption of the commodity belongs not to the seller, but to the buyer. To you, therefore, belongs the use of my daily labour-power. But by means of the price that you pay for it each day, I must be able to reproduce it daily, and to sell it again. I will, like a sensible saving owner, husband my sole wealth, labour-power, and abstain from all foolish waste of it. I will each day spend, set in motion, put into action only as much of it as is compatible with its normal duration, and healthy development. By an unlimited extension of the working day, you may in one day use up a quantity of labour-power greater than I can restore in three. What you gain in labour I lose in substance. The use of my labour-power and the spoliation of it are quite different things. If the average time that (doing a reasonable amount of work) an average labourer can live, is 30 years, the value of my labour-power which you pay me from day to day is $\frac{1}{365 \times 30}$ or $\frac{1}{10950}$ of its total value. But if you consume it in ten years, you pay me daily $\frac{1}{10950}$ instead of $\frac{1}{3650}$ of its total value, i.e., only ⅓ of its daily value, and you rob me, therefore, every day of ⅔ of the value of my commodity. You pay me for one day's labour-power, whilst you use that of 3 days. That is against our contract and the law of exchanges. I demand, therefor, a working day of normal length, and I demand it without any appeal to your heart. You may be a model citizen ; but the thing that you represent face to face with me has no heart in its breast.

We see then, that, apart from extremely elastic bounds, the nature of the exchange of commodities itself imposes no limit to the working day, no limit to surplus-labour. The capitalist maintains his rights as a purchaser when he tries to make the working day as long as possible, and to make, whenever possible, two working days out of one. On the other hand, the peculiar nature of the commodity sold implies a limit to its consumption by the purchaser, and the labourer maintains his right as seller when he wishes to reduce the working day to one of definite normal duration. There is here, therefore, an antinomy, right against right, both equally bearing the seal of the law of exchanges. Between equal rights force decides. Hence is it that in the history of capitalist production, the determination of what is a working day presents itself as the result of a struggle, a struggle between collective capital, *i.e.*, the class of capitalists, and collective labour, *i.e.*, the working class.

Capital has not invented surplus-labour. Wherever a part of society possesses the monopoly of the means of production, the labourer free or not free, must add to the working time necessary for his own maintenance an extra working time in order to produce the means of subsistence for the owners of the means of production, whether this proprietor be the Athenian nobleman, Etruscan theocrat, civis Romanus, Norman baron, American slave owner, Wallachian Boyard, modern landlord or capitalist. Hence in antiquity overwork becomes horrible only when the object is to obtain exchange value in its specific independent money-form ; in the production of gold and silver. Compulsory working to death is here the recognized form of overwork.

But as soon as people, whose production still moves within the lower forms of slave-labour, corvée-labour, &c., are drawn into the whirlpool of an international market dominated by the capitalistic mode of production, the sale of their products for export becoming their principal interest, the civilized horrors of overwork are grafted on the barbaric horrors of slavery, serfdom, &c. Hence the negro labour in the Southern States of the American Union preserved something of a patriarchal character, so long as production was chiefly directed to immediate local consumption. But in proportion, as the export of cotton became of vital interest to these states, the over-working of the negro and sometimes the using up of his life in 7 years of labour became a factor in a calculated and calculating system.

Nothing is from this point of view more characteristic than the designation of the workers who work full time as "full-timers," and the children under 13 who are only allowed to work 6 hours as "half-timers." The worker is here nothing more than personified labour-time. All individual distinctions are merged in those of "full-timers" and "half-timers." To appropriate labour during all the 24 hours of the day is the inherent tendency of capitalist production.

"What is a working day? What is the length of time during which capital may consume the labour-power whose daily value it buys? How far may the working day be extended beyond the working time necessary for the reproduction of labour-power itself?" It has been seen that to these questions capital replies : the working day contains the full 24 hours, with the deduction of the few hours of repose without which labour-power absolutely refuses its services again. Hence it is self-evident that the labourer is nothing else, his whole life through, than labour-power, that therefore all his disposable time is by nature and law labour-time, to be devoted to the self-expansion of capital. Time for education, for intellectual development, for the fulfilling of social functions and for social intercourse, for the free-play of his bodily and mental activity, even the rest time of Sunday (and that in a country of Sabbatarians !) — moonshine !

In its blind unrestrainable passion, its were-wolf hunger for surplus-labour, capital oversteps not only the moral, but even the merely physical maximum bounds of the working day. It usurps the time for growth, development, and healthy maintenance of the body. It steals the time required for the consumption of fresh air and sunlight. It higgles over a meal-time, incorporating it where possible with the process of production itself, so that food is given to the labourer as to a mere means of production, as coal is supplied to the boiler, grease and oil to the machinery. It reduces the sound sleep needed for the restoration, reparation, refresh-

ment of the bodily powers to just so many hours of
torpor as the revival of an organism, absolutely ex-
hausted, renders essential. It is not the normal maintenance of the labour-power which is to determine the
limits of the working day ; it is the greatest possible
daily expenditure of labour-power, no matter how dis-
eased, compulsory, and painful it may be, which is to
determine the limits of the labourers' period of repose.
Capital cares nothing for the length of life of labour-
power. All that concerns it is simply and solely the
maximum of labor-power, that can be rendered fluent
in a working day. It attains this end by shortening the
extent of the labourer's life, as a greedy farmer snatches
increased produce from the soil by robbing it of its
fertility. The capitalistic mode of production (essentially the production of surplus-value, the absorption of
surplus-labour) produces thus, with the extension of
the working day, not only the deterioration of human
labour-power by robbing it of its normal, moral, and
physical conditions of development and function. It
produces also the premature exhaustion and death of
this labour-power itself. It extends the labourer's time
of production during a given period by shortening his
actual life-time.

It takes centuries ere the "free" labourer, thanks to
the development of capitalistic production, agrees, *i.e.*,
is compelled by social conditions, to sell the whole of
his active life, his very capacity for work, for the price
of the necessaries of life, his birthright for a mess of
pottage. Hence it is natural that the lengthening of the
working day, which capital, from the middle of the 14th
to the end of the 17th century, tries to impose by State-
measures on adult labourers, approximately coincides
with the shortening of the working day which, in the
second half of the 19th century, has here and there been
effected by the State to prevent the coining of children's
blood into capital.

The establishment of a normal working day is the result of centuries of struggle between capitalist and labourer.

The first "Statute of Labourers" (23 Edward III, 1349) found its immediate pretext (not its cause) in the great plague that decimated the people, so that, as a Tory writer says, "The difficulty of getting men to work on reasonable terms grew to such a height as to be quite intolerable." Reasonable wages were, therefore, fixed by law as well as the limits of the working day. After capital had taken centuries in extending the working day to its normal maximum limit, and then beyond this to the limit of the natural day of 12 hours, there followed, on the birth of machinism and modern industry in the last third of the 18th century, a violent encroachment like that of an avalanche in its intensity and extent. All bounds of morals and nature, age and sex, day and night, were broken down. Capital celebrated its orgies.

As soon as the working class, stunned at first by the noise and turmoil of the new system of production, recovered, in some measure, its senses, its resistance began, and first in the native land of machinism, in England. For 30 years, however, the concessions conquered by the workpeople were purely nominal. Parliament passed 5 Labour Laws between 1802 and 1833, but was shrewd enough not to vote a penny for their carrying out, for the requisite officials, &c. They remained a dead letter. "The fact is, that prior to the Act of 1833, young persons and children were worked all night, all day, or both *ad libitum.*"

A normal working day for modern industry only dates from the Factory Act of 1833. Nothing is more characteristic of the spirit of capital than the history of the English Factory Acts from 1833 to 1864!

The Act of 1833 declares the ordinary factory working day to be from half-past five in the morning to half-past eight in the evening, and within these limits, a period of 15 hours, it is lawful to employ young persons between 13 and 18 years of age, at any time of the day, provided no one individual young person should work more than 12 hours in any one day, except in certain cases especially provided for.

The law-makers were so far from wishing to trench on the freedom of capital to exploit adult labour-power, or, as they called it, "the freedom of labour," that they created a special system in order to prevent the Factory Acts from having a consequence so outrageous. "The great evil of the factory system as at present conducted," says the first report of the Central Board of the Commission of June 28th, 1833, "has appeared to us to be that it entails the necessity of continuing the labour of children to the utmost length of that of the adults. The only remedy for this evil, short of the limitation of the labour of adults, which would, in our opinion, create an evil greater than that which is sought to be remedied, appears to be the plan of working double sets of children." . . . Under the name of System of Relays, this "plan" was therefore carried out.

In order to reward the manufacturers for having, in the most barefaced way, ignored all the Acts as to children's labour passed during the last twenty-two years, Parliament decreed that after March 1st, 1834, no child under 11, after March 1st, 1835, no child under 12, and after March 1st, 1836, no child under 13, was to work more than eight hours in a factory. That same "reformed" Parliament, which in its delicate consideration for the manufacturers, condemned children under 13, for years to come, to 72 hours of work per week in the Factory Hell, on the other hand, forbade the planters, from the outset, to work any negro slave more than 45 hours a week.

The years 1846–47 are epoch-making in the economic history of England. The Repeal of the Corn Laws, and of the duties on cotton and other raw material ; free trade proclaimed as the guiding star of legislation ; in a word, the arrival of the millennium. On the other hand, in the same years, the Chartist movement and the 10 hours' agitation reached their highest point. The Ten Hours' Act came into force May 1st, 1848. To understand we must remember that none of the Factory Acts of 1833, 1844, and 1847 limited the working day of the male worker over 18, and that since 1833 the 15 hours from 5.30 a.m. to 8.30 p.m. had remained the legal "day," within the limits of which at first the 12 and later the 10 hours' labour of young persons and women had to be performed under the prescribed conditions.

The passion of capital for an unlimited and reckless extension of the working day, is first gratified in the industries earliest revolutionised by water-power, steam, and machinery, cotton, wool, flax, and silk spinning, and weaving. The changes in the material mode of production, and the corresponding changes in the social relations of the producers gave rise first to an extravagance beyond all bounds, and then in opposition to this, called forth a control on the part of Society which legally limits, regulates, and makes uniform the working day and its pauses. This control appears, therefore, during the first half of the nineteenth century simply as exceptional legislation.

The history of the regulation of the working day in certain branches of production, and the struggle still going on in others in regard to this regulation, prove conclusively that the isolated labourer, the labourer as "free" vendor of his labour-power, when capitalist production has once attained a certain stage, succumbs without any power of resistance. The creation of a normal working day is, therefore, the product of a protracted civil war, more or less dissembled, between the capitalist class and the working class. The English factory workers were the champions, not only of the Eng-

lish, but of the modern working class generally, as their
theorists were the first to throw down the gauntlet to
the theory of capital.

France limps slowly behind England. The February
revolution was necessary to bring into the world the
12 hours' law, which is much more deficient than its
English original. For all that, the French revolutionary
method has its special advantages.

In the United States of North America, every independent movement of the workers was paralysed so
long as slavery disfigured a part of the Republic. Labour cannot emancipate itself in the white skin where in
the black it is branded. But out of the death of slavery
a new life at once arose. The first fruit of the Civil War
was the eight hours' agitation, that ran with the seven-
leagued boots of the locomotive from the Atlantic to
the Pacific, from New England to California. For "protection" against "the serpent of their agonies," the labourers must put their heads together, and, as a class,
compel the passing of a law, an all-powerful social bar-
rier that shall prevent the very workers from selling, by
voluntary contract with capital, themselves and their
families into slavery and death. In place of the pompous
catalogue of the "inalienable rights of man" comes the
modest Magna Charta of a legally limited working day.

9. *Rate and Mass of Surplus-Value*

With the rate there is given at the same time the mass
of the surplus-value that the individual labourer fur-
nishes to the capitalist in a definite period of time. If,
e.g., the necessary labour amounts to 6 hours daily, expressed in a quantum of gold $= 3$ shillings, then $3s.$ is
the daily value of one labour-power or the value of the
capital advanced in the buying of one labour-power. If,
further, the rate of surplus-value be $= 100\%$, this variable capital of $3s.$ produces a mass of surplus-value of $3s.$,
or the labourer supplies daily a mass of surplus-labour
equal to 6 hours.

The mass of the surplus-value produced is equal to the amount of the variable capital advanced, multiplied by the rate of surplus-value ; in other words : it is determined by the compound ratio between the number of labour-powers exploited simultaneously by the same capitalist and the degree of exploitation of each individual labour-power.

In the production of a definite mass of surplus-value, the decrease of one factor may be compensated by the increase of the other.

Diminution of the variable capital may therefore be compensated by a proportionate rise in the degree of exploitation of labour-power, or the decrease in the number of the labourers employed by a proportionate extension of the working day. Within certain limits therefore the supply of labour exploitable by capital is independent of the supply of labourers. On the contrary, a fall in the rate of surplus-value leaves unaltered the mass of the surplus-value produced, if the amount of the variable capital, or number of the labourers employed, increases in the same proportion.

Nevertheless, the compensation of a decrease in the number of labourers employed, or of the amount of variable capital advanced, by a rise in the rate of surplus-value, or by the lengthening of the working day, has impassable limits. The absolute limit of the average working day — this being by Nature always less than 24 hours — sets an absolute limit to the compensation of a reduction of variable capital by a higher rate of surplus-value, or of the decrease of the number of labourers exploited by a higher degree of exploitation of labour-power.

The masses of value and of surplus-value produced by different capitals — the value of labour-power being given and its degree of exploitation being equal — vary directly as the amounts of the variable constituents of these capitals, *i.e.*, as their constituents transformed into living labour-power.

Not every sum of money, or of value, is at pleasure transformable into capital. To effect this transformation, in fact, a certain minimum of money or of exchange-value must be presupposed in the hands of the individual possessor of money or commodities. The minimum of variable capital is the cost price of a single labour-power, employed day in, day out, for the production of surplus-value. If this labourer were in possession of his own means of production, and were satisfied to live as a labourer, he need not work beyond the time necessary for the reproduction of his means of subsistence, say 8 hours a day. He would, besides, only require the means of production sufficient for 8 working hours. The capitalist, on the other hand, who makes him do, besides these 8 hours, say 4 hours' surplus-labour, requires an additional sum of money for furnishing the additional means of production. On our supposition, however, he would have to employ two labourers in order to live, on the surplus-value appropriated daily, as well as, and no better than a labourer, *i.e.*, to be able to satisfy his necessary wants. In this case the mere maintenance of life would be the end of his production, not the increase of wealth ; but this latter is implied in capitalist production. That he may live only twice as well as an ordinary labourer, and besides turn half of the surplus-value into capital, he would have to raise, with the number of labourers, the minimum of the capital advanced 8 times. Of course he can take to work himself, participate directly in the process of production, but he is then only a hybrid between capitalist and labourer, a "small master." A certain stage of production necessitates that the capitalist be able to devote the whole of the time during which he functions as a capitalist, *i.e.*, as personified capital, to the appropriation and therefore control of the labour of others, and to the selling of the products of this labour.

Within the process of production, as we have seen, capital acquired the command over labour. The capitalist takes care that the labourer does his work regularly and with the proper degree of intensity.

Capital further developed into a coercive relation, which compels the working class to do more work than the narrow round of its own life-wants prescribes. As a producer of the activity of others, as a pumper-out of surplus-labour and exploiter of labour-power, it surpasses in energy, disregard of bounds, recklessness and efficiency, all earlier systems of production based on directly compulsory labour.

It is now no longer the labourer that employs the means of production, but the means of production that employ the labourer. Instead of being consumed by him as material elements of his productive activity, they consume him as the ferment necessary to their own life-process, and the life-process of capital consists only in its movement as value constantly expanding, constantly multiplying itself.

IV. Production of Relative Surplus-Value

10. *The Concept of Relative Surplus-Value*

Hitherto in treating of surplus-value, arising from a simple prolongation of the working day, we have assumed the mode of production to be given and invariable. But when surplus-value has to be produced by the conversion of necessary labour into surplus-labour, it by no means suffices for capital to take over the labour-process in the form under which it has been historically handed down, and then simply to prolong the duration of that process. The technical and social conditions of the process, and consequently the very mode of production must be revolutionised, before the productiveness of labour can be increased. By that means alone can the value of labour-power be made to sink, and the portion of the working day necessary for the reproduction of that value, be shortened.

The surplus-value produced by prolongation of the

working day, I call *absolute surplus-value*. On the other hand, the surplus-value arising from the curtailment of the necessary labour-time, and from the corresponding alteration in the respective lengths of the two components of the working day, I call *relative surplus-value*.

The shortening of the working day is by no means what is aimed at, in capitalist production, when labour is economised by increasing its productiveness. It is only the shortening of the labour-time, necessary for the production of a definite quantity of commodities, that is aimed at.

The capitalist who applies the improved method of production appropriates to surplus-labour a greater portion of the working day, than the other capitalists in the same trade. On the other hand, however, this extra surplus-value vanishes, so soon as the new method of production has become general and has consequently caused the difference between the individual value of the cheapened commodity and its social value to vanish.

The law of the determination of value by labour-time, a law which brings under its sway the individual capitalist who applies the new method of production, by compelling him to sell his goods under their social value, this same law, acting as a coercive law of competition, forces his competitors to adopt the new method.

In order to effect a fall in the value of labour-power, the increase in the productiveness of labour must seize upon those branches of industry, whose products determine the value of labour-power, and consequently either belong to the class of customary means of subsistence, or are capable of supplying the place of those means. The value of commodities is in inverse ratio to the productiveness of labour. And so, too, is the value of labour-power, because it depends on the values of commodities. Relative surplus-value is, on the contrary, directly proportional to that productiveness. The cheapened commodity, of course, causes only a *pro tanto* fall in the value of labour-power, a fall proportional to the extent of that commodity's employment in the reproduction of labour-power.

11. *Co-operation*

A greater number of labourers working together, at the same time, in one place (or, if you will, in the same field of labour), in order to produce the same sort of commodity under the mastership of one capitalist, constitutes, both historically and logically, the starting point of capitalist production.

When numerous labourers work together side by side, whether in one and the same process, or in different but connected processes, they are said to co-operate, or to work in co-operation.

In every industry, each individual labourer, be he Peter or Paul, differs from the average labourer. These individual differences, or "errors" as they are called in mathematics, compensate one another, and vanish, whenever a certain minimum number of workmen are employed together.

Even without an alteration in the system of working, the simultaneous employment of a large number of labourers effects a revolution in the material conditions of the labour-process. The buildings in which they work, the store-houses for the raw material, the implements and utensils used simultaneously or in turns by the workmen ; in short, a portion of the means of production are now consumed in common. On the one hand, the exchange-value of these means of production is not increased ; for the exchange-value of a commodity is not raised by its use-value being consumed more thoroughly and to greater advantage. On the other hand, they are used in common, and therefore on a larger scale than before. A room where twenty weavers work at twenty looms must be larger than the room of a single weaver with two assistants. But it costs less labour to build one workshop for twenty persons than to build ten to accommodate two weavers each ; thus the value of the means of production that are concentrated for use in common on a large scale does not increase in direct proportion to the expansion and to the increased useful effect of those means. When consumed in common, they give up a smaller part of their value to each single product. Owing to this, the value of a part of the constant capital falls, and in proportion to the magnitude of the fall, the total value of the commodity also falls. The effect is the same as if the means of production had cost less.

Just as the offensive power of a squadron of cavalry, or the defensive power of a regiment of infantry, is essentially different from the sum of the offensive or defensive powers of the individual cavalry or infantry soldiers taken separately, so the sum total of the mechanical forces exerted by isolated workmen differs from the social force that is developed, when many hands take part simultaneously in one and the same undivided operation.

Not only have we here an increase in the productive power of the individual, by means of co-operation, but the creation of a new power, namely, the collective power of masses.

Apart from the new power that arises from the fusion of many forces into one single force, mere social contact begets in most industries an emulation and a stimulation of the animal spirits that heighten the efficiency of each individual workman. Hence it is that a dozen persons working together will, in their collective working day of 144 hours, produce far more than twelve isolated men each working 12 hours, or than one man who works twelve days in succession. The reason of this is that a man is, if not as Aristotle contends, a political, at all events a social animal.

Although a number of men may be occupied together

at the same time on the same or the same kind of work,
yet the labour of each, as a part of the collective labour, may correspond to a distinct phase of the labour-
process, through all whose phases, in consequence of
co-operation, the subject of their labour passes with
greater speed. For instance, if a dozen masons place
themselves in a row, so as to pass stones from the foot
of a ladder to its summit, each of them does the same
thing ; nevertheless, their separate acts form connected
parts of one total operation ; they are particular phases,
which must be gone through by each stone ; and the
stones are thus carried up quicker by the 24 hands of the
row of them than they could be if each man went separately up and down the ladder with his burden. The
object is carried over the same distance in a shorter time.
Again, a combination of labour occurs whenever a
building, for instance, is taken in hand on different sides
simultaneously ; although here also the co-operating
masons are doing the same or the same kind of work.

If the work be complicated, then the mere number of
the men who co-operate allows of the various operations being apportioned to different hands, and, consequently, of being carried on simultaneously. The time
necessary for the completion of the whole work is
thereby shortened.

On the one hand, co-operation allows of the work being carried on over an extended space ; it is consequently
imperatively called for in certain undertakings. On the
other hand, while extending the scale of production, it
renders possible a relative contraction of the arena,
whereby a number of useless expenses are cut down.

The number of the labourers that co-operate, or the
scale of co-operation, depends, in the first instance, on
the amount of capital that the individual capitalist can
spare for the purchase of labour-power ; in other words,
on the extent to which a single capitalist has command
over the means of subsistence of a number of labourers.
And as with the variable, so it is with the constant

capital. Hence, concentration of large masses of the means of production in the hands of individual capitalists, is a material condition for the co-operation of wage-labourers, and the extent of the co-operation or the scale of production, depends on the extent of this concentration.

That a capitalist should command on the field of production, is now as indispensable as that a general should command on the field of battle. All combined labour on a large scale requires, more or less, a directing authority, in order to secure the harmonious working of the individual activities, and to perform the general functions that have their origin in the action of the combined organism, as distinguished from the action of its separate organs. A single violin player is his own conductor ; an orchestra requires a separate one. The work of directing, superintending, and adjusting becomes one of the functions of capital, from the moment that the labour under the control of capital becomes co-operative. Once a function of capital, it acquires special characteristics.

When the labourer co-operates systematically with others, he strips off the fetters of his individuality, and develops the capabilities of his species.

The connexion existing between their various labours appears to them, ideally, in the shape of a preconceived plan of the capitalist, and practically in the shape of the authority of the same capitalist, in the shape of the powerful will of another, who subjects their activity to his aims.

As the number of the co-operating labourers increases, so too does their resistance to the domination of capital, and with it, the necessity for capital to overcome this resistance by counter-pressure. The control exercised by the capitalist is not only a special function, due to the nature of the social labour-process, and peculiar to that process, but it is, at the same time, a function of the exploitation of a social labour-process, and is consequently rooted in the unavoidable antagonism between the exploiter and the living and labouring raw material he exploits.

If the control of the capitalist is in substance twofold by reason of the twofold nature of the process of production itself, in form that control is despotic. So soon as capital has reached that minimum amount with which capitalist production as such begins, he hands over the work of direct and constant supervision of the individual workmen, and groups of workmen, to a special kind of wage labourer. An industrial army of workmen requires, like a real army, officers (managers), and sergeants (foremen, overlookers) who, while the work is being done, command in the name of the capitalist. It is not because he is a leader of industry that a man is a capitalist ; on the contrary, he is a leader of industry because he is a capitalist. The leadership of industry is an attribute of capital, just as in feudal times the functions of general and judge were attributes of landed property.

The productive power developed by the labourer when working in co-operation, is the productive power of capital. This power is developed gratuitously, whenever the workmen are placed under given conditions, and it is capital that places them under such conditions. Because this power costs capital nothing, and because, on the other hand, the labourer himself does not develop it before his labour belongs to capital, it appears as a power with which capital is endowed by Nature — a productive power that is immanent in capital.

Co-operation, such as we find it at the dawn of human development, is based, on the one hand, on ownership in common of the means of production, and on the other hand, on the fact that, in those cases, each individual has no more torn himself off from the navelstring of his tribe or community, than each bee has freed itself from connexion with the hive. Such co-operation is distinguished from capitalistic co-operation by both of the above characteristics. The sporadic application

of co-operation on a large scale in ancient times, in the
Middle Ages, and in modern colonies, reposes on relations of dominion and servitude, principally on slavery.
The capitalistic form, on the contrary, presupposes
from first to last the free wage labourer, who sells
his labour-power to capital. Historically, however, this
form is developed in opposition to peasant agriculture
and to the carrying on of independent handicrafts.
From the standpoint of these, capitalistic co-operation
does not manifest itself as a particular historical form of
co-operation, but co-operation itself appears to be a
historical form peculiar to, and specifically distinguish-
ing, the capitalist process of production.

Co-operation is the first change experienced by the
actual labour-process, when subjected to capital. This
change takes place spontaneously. The simultaneous
employment of a large number of wage-labourers, in
one and the same process, forms the starting point of
capitalist production, and is a necessary concomitant.

12. *Division of Labour and Manufacture*

That co-operation which is based on division of labour assumes its typical form in the manufacture, and
is the prevalent characteristic form of the capitalist
process of production throughout the manufacturing
period properly so called. That period, roughly speaking, extends from the middle of the 16th to the last
third of the 18th century.

Manufacture takes its rise in two ways : By the assemblage, in one workshop under the control of a single
capitalist, of labourers belonging to various independent
handicrafts, but through whose hands a given article
must pass on its way to completion. As an example of
that kind we may take a watch. Formerly the individual work of an artificer, the watch has been transformed
into the social product of an immense number of detail
labourers, and all these come together for the first time
in the hand that binds them into one mechanical whole.

Manufacture also arises in a way exactly the reverse of this — namely, by one capitalist employing simultaneously in one workshop a number of artificers, who all do the same or the same kind of work. The work is redistributed. Instead of each man being allowed to perform all the various operations in succession, these operations are changed into disconnected, isolated ones, carried on side by side ; each is assigned to a different artificer, and the whole of them together are performed simultaneously by the co-operating workmen. The commodity, from being the individual product of an independent artificer, becomes the social product of a union of artificers. This perfected form produces articles that go through connected phases of development, through a series of processes step by step, like the wire in the manufacture of needles, which passes through the hands of 72 and sometimes even 92 different detail workmen.

The mode in which manufacture arises, its growth out of handicrafts, is therefore twofold. On the one hand, it arises from the union of various independent handicrafts, which become stripped of their independence and specialised to such an extent as to be reduced to mere supplementary partial processes in the production of one particular commodity. On the other hand, it arises from the co-operation of artificers of one handicraft ; it splits up that particular handicraft into its various detail operations, isolating, and making these operations independent of one another up to the point where each becomes the exclusive function of a particular labourer. On the one hand, therefore, manufacture either introduces division of labour into a process of production, or further developes that division ; on the other hand, it unites together handicrafts that were formerly separate. But whatever may have been its particular starting point, its final form is invariably the same — a productive mechanism whose parts are human beings.

Whether complex or simple, each operation has to be done by hand, retains the character of a handicraft, and is therefore dependent on the strength, skill, quickness, and sureness of the individual workman in handling his tools. The handicraft continues to be the basis. This narrow technical basis excludes a really scientific analysis of any definite process of industrial production, since it is still a condition that each detail process gone through by the product must be capable of being done by hand and of forming, in its way, a separate handicraft. It is just because handicraft skill continues, in this way, to be the foundation of the process of production, that each workman becomes exclusively assigned to a partial function, and that for the rest of his life, his labour-power is turned into the organ of this detail function.

It is clear that a labourer who all his life performs one and the same simple operation, converts his whole body into the automatic, specialised implement of that operation. Consequently, he takes less time in doing it, than the artificer who performs a whole series of operations in succession. But the collective labourer is made up solely of such specialised detail labourers. Hence, in comparison with the independent handicraft, more is produced in a given time, or the productive power of labour is increased.

Moreover, when once this fractional work is established as the exclusive function of one person, the methods it employs become perfected. The workman's continued repetition of the same simple act, and the concentration of his attention on it, teach him by experience how to attain the desired effect with the minimum of exertion. But since there are always several generations of labourers living at one time, and working together at the manufacture of a given article, the technical skill, the tricks of the trade thus acquired, become established, and are accumulated and handed down.

Manufacture, in fact, produces the skill of the detail

labourer, by reproducing, and systematically driving to an extreme within the workshop, the naturally developed differentiation of trades, which it found ready to hand in society at large. On the other hand, the conversion of fractional work into the life-calling of one man corresponds to the tendency shown by earlier societies to make trades hereditary ; either to petrify them into castes, or whenever definite historical conditions beget in the individual a tendency to vary in a manner incompatible with the nature of castes, to ossify them into guilds.

An artificer, who performs one after another the various fractional operations in the production of a finished article, must at one time change his place, at another his tools. The transition from one operation to another interrupts the flow of his labour, and creates, so to say, gaps in his working day. These gaps close up so soon as he is tied to one and the same operation all day long ; they vanish in proportion as the changes in his work diminish. The resulting increased productive power is owing either to an increased expenditure of labour-power in a given time — *i.e.*, to increased intensity of labour — or to a decrease in the amount of labour-power unproductively consumed.

The productiveness of labour depends not only on the proficiency of the workman, but on the perfection of his tools. Alterations become necessary in the implements that previously served more than one purpose. The direction taken by this change is determined by the difficulties experienced in consequence of the unchanged form of the implement. Manufacture is characterized by the differentiation of the instruments of labour — a differentiation whereby implements of a given sort acquire fixed shapes, adapted to each particular application, and by the specialisation of those instruments, giving to each special instrument its full play only in the hands of a specific detail labourer.

In so far as a manufacture, when first started, com-

bines scattered handicrafts, it lessens the space by which
the various phases of production are separated from
each other. The time taken in passing from one stage
to another is shortened, so is the labour that effectuates
this passage. In comparison with a handicraft, productive power is gained. On the other hand, division
of labour, which is the principle of manufacture, requires the isolation of the various stages of production
and their independence of each other. The establishment and maintenance of a connexion between the isolated functions necessitates the incessant transport of
the article from one hand to another, and from one
process to another. From the standpoint of modern mechanical industry, this necessity stands forth as a characteristic and costly disadvantage, and one that is immanent in the principle of manufacture.

Since the fractional product of each detail labourer
is, at the same time, only a particular stage in the development of one and the same finished article, each
labourer, or each group of labourers, prepares the raw
material for another labourer or group. The result of
the labour of the one is the starting point for the labour
of the other. The one workman therefore gives occupa-
tion directly to the other. The labour-time necessary
in each partial process, for attaining the desired effect,
is learnt by experience ; and the mechanism of Manufacture, as a whole, is based on the assumption that a
given result will be obtained in a given time. It is only on
this assumption that the various supplementary labour-
processes can proceed uninterruptedly, simultaneously,
and side by side.

This direct dependence of the operations, and therefore of the labourers, on each other, compels each one
of them to spend on his work no more than the necessary time, and thus a continuity, uniformity, regularity,
order, and even intensity of labour, of quite a different
kind, is begotten than is to be found in an independent
handicraft or even in simple co-operation. The rule

that the labour-time expended on a commodity should
not exceed that which is socially necessary for its production, appears, in the production of commodities generally, to be established by the mere effect of competition ; since, to express ourselves superficially, each single
producer is obliged to sell his commodity at its market
price. In Manufacture, on the contrary, the turning out
of a given quantum of product in a given time is a
technical law of the process of production itself.

The division of labour, as carried out in the Manufacture, not only simplifies and multiplies the qualitatively different parts of the social collective labourer,
but also creates a fixed mathematical relation or ratio
which regulates the quantitative extent of those parts —
i.e., the relative number of labourers, or the relative
size of the group of labourers, for each detail operation.
It developes, along with the qualitative sub-division of
the social labour process, a quantitative rule and pro-
portionality for that process.

Early in the manufacturing period, the principle of
lessening the necessary labour-time in the production
of commodities was accepted and formulated : and the
use of machines, especially for certain simple first processes that have to be conducted on a very large scale,
and with the application of great force, sprang up here
and there. But, on the whole, machinery played that
subordinate part which Adam Smith assigns to it in
comparison with division of labour.

The collective labourer, formed by the combination
of a number of detail labourers, is the mechanism specially characteristic of the manufacturing period. The
various operations that are performed in turns by the
producer of a commodity, and coalesce one with another during the progress of production, lay claim to
him in various ways. In one operation he must exert
more strength, in another more skill, in another more
attention ; and the same individual does not possess all
these qualities in an equal degree. After Manufacture

has once separated, made independent, and isolated the various operations, the labourers are divided, classified, and grouped according to their predominating qualities. If their natural endowments are, on the one hand, the foundation on which the division of labour is built up, on the other hand, Manufacture, once introduced, developes in them new powers that are by nature fitted only for limited and special functions. The collective labourer now possesses, in an equal degree of excellence, all the qualities requisite for production, and expends them in the most economical manner, by exclusively employing all his organs, consisting of particular labourers, or groups of labourers, in performing their special functions. The one-sidedness and the deficiencies of the detail labourer become perfections when he is a part of the collective labourer. The habit of doing only one thing converts him into a never failing instrument, while his connexion with the whole mechanism compels him to work with the regularity of the parts of a machine.

Since the collective labourer has functions, both simple and complex, both high and low, his members, the individual labour-powers, require different degrees of training, and must therefore have different values. Manufacture, therefore, developes a hierarchy of labour-powers, to which there corresponds a scale of wages.

Furthermore, manufacture begets, in every handicraft that it seizes upon, a class of so-called unskilled labourers, a class which handicraft industry strictly excluded. If it developes a one-sided specialty into a perfection, at the expense of the whole of a man's working capacity, it also begins to make a specialty of the absence of all development. Alongside of the hierarchic gradation there steps the simple separation of the labourers into skilled and unskilled. For the latter, the cost of apprenticeship vanishes ; for the former, it diminishes. The fall in the value of labour-power, caused by the disappearance or diminution of the expense of apprenticeship, implies a direct increase of surplus-value for the benefit of capital ; for everything that shortens the necessary labour-time required for the reproduction of labour-power, extends the domain of surplus-labour.

The mechanism that is made up of numerous individual detail labourers belongs to the capitalist. Hence, the productive power resulting from a combination of labourers appears to be the productive power of capital.

If, at first, the workman sells his labour-power to capital, because the material means of producing a commodity fail him, now his very labour-power refuses its services unless it has been sold to capital. Its functions can be exercised only in an environment that exists in the workshop of the capitalist after the sale. By nature unfitted to make anything independently, the manufacturing labourer developes productive activity as a mere appendage of the capitalist's workshop. As the chosen people bore in their features the sign manual of Jehovah, so division of labour brands the manufacturing workman as the property of capital.

In order to make the collective labourer, and through him capital, rich in social productive power, each labourer must be made poor in individual productive powers. As a matter of fact, some few manufacturers in the middle of the 18th century preferred, for certain operations that were trade secrets, to employ half-idiotic persons. Some crippling of body and mind is inseparable even from division of labour in society as a whole. However, manufacture is the first to afford the materials for, and to give a start to, industrial pathology.

Division of labour in manufacture creates new conditions for the lordship of capital over labour. If, therefore, on the one hand, it presents itself historically as a progress and as a necessary phase in the economic development of society, on the other hand it is a refined and civilised method of exploitation.

Hence throughout the whole manufacturing period there runs the complaint of want of discipline among the workmen. Capital is constantly compelled to wrestle with the insubordination of the workmen. Capital failed to become the master of the whole disposable working-time of the manufacturing labourers.

Manufacture was unable either to seize upon the production of society to its full extent, or to revolutionise that production to its very core. It towered up as an economical work of art on the broad foundation of the town handicrafts, and of the rural domestic industries. At a given stage in its development, the narrow technical basis on which manufacture rested came into conflict with requirements of production that were created by manufacture itself.

One of its most finished creations was the workshop for the production of the instruments of labour themselves, including especially the complicated mechanical apparatus then already employed. This workshop, the product of the division of labour in manufacture, produced in its turn — machines.

13. *Machinery and Modern Industry*

In manufacture, the revolution in the mode of production begins with the labour-power, in modern industry it begins with the instruments of labour. Our first inquiry then is, how the instruments of labour are converted from tools into machines, or what is the difference between a machine and the implements of a handicraft ?

All fully developed machinery consists of three essentially different parts, the motor mechanism, the transmitting mechanism, and finally the tool or working machine. The motor mechanism is that which puts the whole in motion. The transmitting mechanism regulates the motion, changes its form where necessary (as, for instance, from linear to circular) and divides and distributes it among the working machines. The tool or working machine is that part of the machinery with which the industrial revolution of the 18th century started. And to this day it constantly serves as such a starting point, whenever a handicraft, or a manufacture, is turned into an industry carried on by machinery.

On a closer examination of the working machine proper, we find in it, as a general rule, though often, no doubt, under very altered forms, the apparatus and tools used by the handicraftsman or manufacturing workman ; with this difference, that instead of being human implements, they are the implements of a mechanism, or mechanical implements. Either the entire machine is only a more or less altered mechanical edition of the old handicraft tool, as, for instance, the power-loom ; or the working parts fitted in the frame of the machine are old acquaintances, as spindles are in a mule, needles in a stocking-loom, saws in a sawing machine, and knives in a chopping machine. The distinction between these tools and the body proper of the machine exists from their very birth ; for they continue for the most part to be produced by handicraft, or by manufacture, and are afterwards fitted into the body of the machine, which is the product of machinery. The machine proper is therefore a mechanism that, after being set in motion, performs with its tools the same operations that were formerly done by the workman with similar tools. Whether the motive power is derived from man, or from some other machine, makes no difference in this respect.

From the moment that the tool proper is taken from man, and fitted into a mechanism, a machine takes the place of a mere implement. The difference strikes one at once, even in those cases where man himself continues to be the prime mover. The number of implements that he himself can use simultaneously is limited by the number of his own natural instruments of production, by the number of his bodily organs. In Germany, they tried at first to make one spinner work

two spinning wheels, that is, to work simultaneously
with both hands and both feet. This was too difficult.
Later, a treadle spinning wheel with two spindles was
invented, but adepts in spinning, who could spin two
threads at once, were almost as scarce as two-headed
men. The Jenny, on the other hand, even at its very
birth, spun with 12–18 spindles, and the stocking-loom
knits with many thousand needles at once. The number of tools that a machine can bring into play simultaneously, is from the very first emancipated from the
organic limits that hedge in the tools of a handicraftsman.

Increase in the size of the machine, and in the number
of its working tools, calls for a more massive mechanism
to drive it ; and this mechanism requires, in order to
overcome its resistance, a mightier moving power than
that of man. Not till the invention of Watt's second
and so-called double-acting steam-engine, was a prime
mover found, that begot its own force by the consumption of coal and water, whose power was entirely under
man's control, that was mobile and a means of locomo-
tion, that was urban and not, like the water-wheel, rural,
that permitted production to be concentrated in towns
instead of, like the water-wheels, being scattered up and
down the country, that was of universal technical application, and, relatively speaking, little affected in its
choice of residence by local circumstances. The greatness of Watt's genius showed itself in the specification
of the patent that he took out in April, 1784. In that
specification his steam-engine is described, not as an
invention for a specific purpose, but as an agent universally applicable in Mechanical Industry.

The motive mechanism grows with the number of the
machines that are turned simultaneously, and the transmitting mechanism becomes a wide-spreading apparatus. We now proceed to distinguish the co-operation
of a number of machines of one kind from a complex
system of machinery. In the one case, the product is

entirely made by a single machine. Whether this be merely a reproduction of one complicated manual implement, or a combination of various simple implements specialised by Manufacture, in either case, in the factory, we meet again with simple co-operation ; and, this co-operation presents itself to us, in the first instance, as the conglomeration in one place of similar and simultaneously acting machines. A real machinery system, however, does not take the place of these independent machines, until the subject of labour goes through a connected series of detail processes, that are carried out by a chain of machines of various kinds, the one supplementing the other. Here we have again the co-operation by division of labour that characterises Manufacture ; only now, it is a combination of detail machines.

The collective machine, now an organised system of various kinds of single machines, and of groups of single machines, becomes more and more perfect, the more the process as a whole becomes a continuous one, *i.e.*, the less the raw material is interrupted in its passage from its first phase to its last ; in other words, the more its passage from one phase to another is effected, not by the hand of man, but by the machinery itself. In Manufacture the isolation of each detail process is a condition imposed by the nature of division of labour, but in the fully developed factory the continuity of those processes is, on the contrary, imperative.

As soon as a machine executes, without man's help, all the movements requisite to elaborate the raw material, needing only attendance from him, we have an automatic system of machinery.

An organised system of machines, to which motion is communicated by the transmitting mechanism from a central automaton, is the most developed form of production by machinery. Here we have, in the place of the isolated machine, a mechanical monster whose body fills whole factories, and whose demon power, at first veiled under the slow and measured motions of his giant limbs, at length breaks out into the fast and furious whirl of his countless working organs.

Just as the individual machine retains a dwarfish character, so long as it is worked by the power of man alone, and just as no system of machinery could be properly developed before the steam engine took the place of the earlier motive powers ; so, too, Modern Industry was crippled in its complete development, so long as its characteristic instrument of production, the machine, owed its existence to personal strength and personal skill.

Machinery operates only by means of associated labour, or labour in common. Hence, the co-operative character of the labour-process is, in the latter case, a technical necessity dictated by the instrument of labour itself. Machinery, like every other component of constant capital, creates no new value, but yields up its own value to the product that it serves to beget. Given the rate at which machinery transfers its value to the product, the amount of value so transferred depends on the total value of the machinery. The less labour it contains, the less value it imparts to the product. The less value it gives up, so much the more productive it is, and so much the more its services approximate to those of natural forces. The productiveness of a machine is therefore measured by the human labour-power it replaces.

The use of machinery for the exclusive purpose of cheapening the product, is limited in this way, that less labour must be expended in producing the machinery than is displaced by the employment of that machinery. For the capitalist, however, this use is still more limited. Instead of paying for the labour, he only pays the value of the labour-power employed ; therefore, the limit to his using a machine is fixed by the difference between the value of the machine and the value of the labour-power replaced by it.

In so far as machinery dispenses with muscular power, it becomes a means of employing labourers of slight muscular strength, and those whose bodily development is incomplete, but whose limbs are all the more supple. The labour of women and children was, therefore, the first thing sought for by capitalists who used machinery.

That mighty substitute for labour and labourers was forthwith changed into a means for increasing the number of wage-labourers by enrolling, under the direct sway of capital, every member of the workman's family, without distinction of age or sex. Compulsory work for the capitalist usurped the place, not only of the children's play, but also of free labour at home within moderate limits for the support of the family.

Machinery, by throwing every member of that family on to the labour market, spreads the value of the man's labour-power over his whole family. It thus depreciates his labour-power. In order that the family may live, four people must now, not only labour, but expend surplus-labour for the capitalist. Thus we see, that machinery, while augmenting the human material that forms the principal object of capital's exploiting power, at the same time raises the degree of exploitation.

Previously, the workman sold his own labour-power, which he disposed of nominally as a free agent. Now he sells wife and child. He has become a slave dealer.

As was shown by an official medical inquiry in the year 1861, the high death-rates are, apart from local causes, principally due to the employment of the mothers away from their homes, and to the neglect and maltreatment consequent on her absence ; beside this, there arises an unnatural estrangement between mother and child, and as a consequence intentional starving and poisoning of the children. In fact, the revolution in the mode of cultivation had led to the introduction of the industrial system. Married women, who work in gangs along with boys and girls, are, for a stipulated sum of money, placed at the disposal of the farmer, by a man called "the undertaker," who contracts for the whole gang. "These gangs will sometimes travel many miles from their own village ; they are to be met morning and evening on the roads." Every phenomenon of the factory districts is here reproduced, including, but to a greater extent, ill-disguised infanticide, and dosing children with opiates.

The moral degradation caused by the capitalistic exploitation of women and children has been so exhaustively depicted by F. Engels in his "Lage der Arbeitenden Klasse Englands," and other writers, that I need only mention the subject in this place.

The spirit of capitalist production stands out clearly in the ludicrous wording of the so-called education clauses in the Factory Acts, in the absence of an administrative machinery, an absence that again makes the compulsion illusory, in the opposition of the manufacturers themselves to these education clauses, and in the tricks and dodges they put in practice for evading them.

If machinery be the most powerful means for increasing the productiveness of labour — *i.e.*, for shortening the working time required in the production of a commodity, it becomes in the hands of capital the most powerful means, in those industries first invaded by it, for lengthening the working day beyond all bounds set by human nature.

The active life-time of a machine is, however, clearly dependent on the length of the working day, or on the duration of the daily labour-process multiplied by the number of days for which the process is carried on.

The material wear and tear of a machine is of two kinds. The one arises from use, as coins wear away by circulating, the other from non-use, as a sword rusts when left in its scabbard.

But in addition to the material wear and tear, a machine also undergoes what we may call a moral depreciation. It loses exchange-value, either by machines of the same sort being produced cheaper than it, or by better machines entering into competition with it. In both cases, its value is determined by the labour-time requisite to reproduce either it or the better machine. It has, therefore, lost value more or less. The shorter the period taken to reproduce its total value, the less is the danger of moral depreciation ; and the longer the working day, the shorter is that period. When machinery is first introduced, new methods of reproducing it more cheaply follow blow upon blow, and so do improvements, that not only affect individual parts and details of the machine, but its entire build. It is, therefore, in the early days of the life of machinery that this special incentive to the prolongation of the working day makes itself felt most acutely.

The development of the factory system fixes a constantly increasing portion of the capital in a form, in which, on the one hand, its value is capable of continual self-expansion, and in which, on the other hand, it loses both use-value and exchange-value whenever it loses contact with living labour. Machinery produces relative surplus-value ; not only by directly depreciating the value of labour-power, and by indirectly cheapening the same through cheapening the commodities that enter into its reproduction, but also, when it is first introduced sporadically into an industry, by converting the labour employed by the owner of that machinery, into labour of a higher degree and greater efficacy, by raising the social value of the article produced above its individual value, and thus enabling the capitalist to replace the value of a day's labour-power by a smaller portion of the value of the day's product. During this transition period, when the use of machinery is a sort of monopoly, the profits are therefore exceptional.

As the use of machinery becomes more general in

a particular industry, the social value of the product sinks down to its individual value, and the law that surplus-value does not arise from the labour-power that has been replaced by the machinery, but from the labour-power actually employed in working with the machinery, asserts itself. It is impossible, for instance, to squeeze as much surplus-value out of 2 as out of 24 labourers. If each of these 24 men gives only one hour of surplus-labour in 12, the 24 men give together 24 hours of surplus-labour, while 24 hours is the total labour of the two men. Hence, the application of machinery to the production of surplus-value implies a contradiction which is immanent in it, since, of the two factors of the surplus-value created by a given amount of capital, one, the rate of surplus-value cannot be increased, except by diminishing the other, the number of workmen.

This contradiction comes to light as soon as by the general employment of machinery in a given industry, the value of the machine-produced commodity regulates the value of all commodities of the same sort ; and it is this contradiction that, in its turn, drives the capitalist, without his being conscious of the fact, to excessive lengthening of the working day, in order that he may compensate the decrease in the relative number of labourers exploited, by an increase not only of the relative, but of the absolute surplus-labour.

If, then, the capitalistic employment of machinery, on the one hand, supplies new and powerful motives to an excessive lengthening of the working day, and radically changes, as well the methods of labour, as also the character of the social working organism, in such a manner as to break down all opposition to this tendency, on the other hand it produces, partly by opening out to the capitalist new strata of the working class, previously inaccessible to him, partly by setting free the labourers it supplants, a surplus working population, which is compelled to submit to the dictation of capital. Hence that remarkable phenomenon in the history of Modern Industry, that machinery sweeps away every moral and natural restriction on the length of the working day. Hence, too, the economical paradox, that the most powerful instrument for shortening labour-time becomes the most unfailing means for placing every moment of the labourer's time and that of his family at the disposal of the capitalist for the purpose of expanding the value of his capital.

It is self-evident, that in proportion as the use of machinery spreads, and the experience of a special class of workmen habituated to machinery accumulates, the rapidity and intensity of labour increase as a natural consequence. Thus in England, during half a century, lengthening of the working day went hand in hand with increasing intensity of factory labour. Nevertheless a point must inevitably be reached, where extension of the working day and intensity of the labour mutually exclude one another, in such a way that lengthening of the working day becomes compatible only with a lower degree of intensity, and a higher degree of intensity only with a shortening of the working day. So soon as the revolt of the working class compelled Parliament to shorten compulsorily the hours of labour, and to begin by imposing a normal working day on factories proper, so soon as an increased production of surplus value by the prolongation of the working day was once for all put a stop to, from that moment capital threw itself with all its might into the production of relative surplus-value, by hastening on the further improvement of machinery.

At the same time a change took place in the nature of relative surplus-value. The denser hour of the ten hours' working day contains more labour, i.e., expended labour-power, than the more porous hour of the twelve hours' working day. The product therefore of one of the former hours has as much or more value than has the product of the latter hours.

How is the labour intensified ?

The first effect of shortening the working day results from the self-evident law, that the efficiency of labour-power is in an inverse ratio to the duration of its expenditure. Hence, within certain limits what is lost by shortening the duration is gained by the increasing tension of labour-power. So soon as that shortening becomes compulsory, machinery becomes in the hands of capital the objective means, systematically employed for squeezing out more labour in a given time. This is effected in two ways : by increasing the speed of the machinery, and by giving the workman more machinery to tend.

Improved construction of the machinery is necessary, partly because without it greater pressure cannot be put on the workman, and partly because the shortened hours of labour force the capitalist to exercise the strictest watch over the cost of production. The improvements in the steam-engine have increased the piston speed, and at the same time have made it possible, by means of a greater economy of power, to drive with the same or even a smaller consumption of coal more machinery with the same engine. The improvements in the transmitting mechanism have lessened friction, have reduced the diameter and weight of the shafting to a constantly decreasing minimum. Finally, the improvements in the operative machines have, while reducing their size, increased their speed and efficiency, as in the modern power-loom ; or, while increasing the size of their frame-work, have also increased the extent and number of their working parts, as in spinning mules, or have added to the speed of these working parts by imperceptible alterations of detail, such as the spindles in self-acting mules.

Along with the tool, the skill of the workman in handling it passes over to the machine. The capabilities of the tool are emancipated from the restraints that are inseparable from human labour-power. Thereby the technical foundation on which is based the division of labour in Manufacture is swept away. Hence, in the place of the hierarchy of specialised workmen that characterises manufacture, there steps, in the automatic factory, a tendency to equalise and reduce to one and the same level every kind of work that has to be done by the minders of the machines ; in the place of the artificially produced differentiations of the detail workmen, step the natural differences of age and sex.

The life-long speciality of handling one and the same tool now becomes the life-long speciality of serving one and the same machine. Machinery is put to a wrong use, with the object of transforming the workman, from his very childhood, into a part of a detail-machine.

At the same time that factory work exhausts the nervous system to the uttermost, it does away with the many-sided play of the muscles, and confiscates every atom of freedom, in both bodily and intellectual activity. The lightening of the labour, even, becomes a sort of torture, since the machine does not free the labourer from work, but deprives the work of all interest. Every kind of capitalist production has this in common, that it is not the workman that employs the instruments of labour, but the instruments of labour that employ the workman. But it is only in the factory system that this inversion for the first time acquires technical and palpable reality. By means of its conversion into an automaton, the instrument of labour confronts the labourer, during the labour-process, in the shape of capital, of dead labour, that dominates, and pumps dry, living labour-power.

The technical subordination of the workman to the uniform motion of the instruments of labour, and the peculiar composition of the body of workpeople, con-sisting as it does of individuals of both sexes and of all ages, give rise to a barrack discipline, which is elaborated into a complete system in the factory, and which fully developes the before mentioned labour of overlooking, thereby dividing the workpeople into operatives and overlookers, into private soldiers and sergeants of an industrial army. The factory code in which capital formulates his autocracy over his workpeople, is but the capitalistic caricature of that social regulation of the labour-process. The place of the slave driver's lash is taken by the overlooker's book of penalties. Is Fourier wrong when he calls factories "tempered bagnios"?

The contest between the capitalist and the wage-labourer dates back to the very origin of capital. It raged on throughout the whole manufacturing period. But only since the introduction of machinery has the workman fought against the instrument of labour itself, the material embodiment of capital. He revolts against this particular form of the means of production, as being the material basis of the capitalist mode of production.

In the 17th century nearly all Europe experienced revolts of the workpeople against the ribbon-loom. A wind-sawmill, erected near London by a Dutchman, succumbed to the excesses of the populace. No sooner had Everet in 1758 erected the first wool-shearing machine that was driven by water-power, than it was set on fire by 100,000 people who had been thrown out of work. The enormous destruction of machinery that occurred in the English manufacturing districts, known as the Luddite movement, gave governments a pretext for the most re-actionary and forcible measures. It took both time and experience before the workpeople learnt to distinguish between machinery and its employment by capital, and to direct their attacks, not against the material instruments of production, but against the mode in which they are used.

The instrument of labour, when it takes the form of a machine, immediately becomes a competitor of the workman himself. When machinery seizes on an industry by degrees, it produces chronic misery among the operatives who compete with it. Where the transition is rapid, the effect is acute and felt by great masses. The instrument of labour strikes down the labourer.

In Modern Industry the continual improvement of machinery and the development of the automatic system have an analogous effect. Who, in 1860, the Zenith year of the English cotton industry, would have dreamt of the galloping improvements in machinery, and the corresponding displacement of working people, called into being during the following 3 years, under the stimulus of the American Civil War? Between 1861 and 1868, the number of spindles increased by 1,612,541, while the number of operatives decreased by 50,505.

Machinery is the most powerful weapon for repressing strikes, those periodical revolts of the working class against the autocracy of capital. The steam-engine was from the very first an antagonist of human power, an antagonist that enabled the capitalist to tread under foot the growing claims of the workmen, who threatened the newly born factory system with a crisis. It would be possible to write quite a history of the inventions, made since 1830, for the sole purpose of supplying capital with weapons against the revolts of the working class.

The contradictions and antagonisms inseparable from the capitalist employment of machinery, do not exist, since they do not arise out of machinery, as such, but out of its capitalist employment! It is an undoubted fact that machinery, as such, is not responsible for "setting free" the workman from the means of subsistence.

In proportion as machinery, with the aid of a relatively small number of workpeople, increases the mass of raw materials, intermediate products, instruments of labour, &c., the working-up of these raw materials and intermediate products becomes split up into numberless branches ; social production increases in diversity. The factory system carries the social division of labour immeasurably further than does manufacture, for it increases the productiveness of the industries it seizes upon, in a far higher degree.

The immediate result of machinery is to augment surplus-value and the mass of products in which surplus-value is embodied. And, as the substances consumed by the capitalists and their dependants become more plentiful, so too do these orders of society. Their growing wealth, and the relatively diminished number of workmen required to produce the necessaries of life beget, simultaneously with the rise of new and luxurious wants, the means of satisfying those wants. A larger portion of the produce of society is changed into surplus produce, and a larger part of the surplus produce is supplied for consumption in a multiplicity of refined shapes. In other words, the production of luxuries increases. Lastly, the extraordinary productiveness of modern industry, accompanied as it is by both a more extensive and a more intense exploitation of labour-power in all other spheres of production, allows of the unproductive employment of a larger and larger part of the working class, and the consequent reproduction, on a constantly extending scale, of the ancient domestic slaves under the name of a servant class.

The increase of the means of production and subsistence, accompanied by a relative diminution in the number of labourers, causes an increased demand for labour in making canals, docks, tunnels, bridges, and so on, works that can only bear fruit in the far future. Entirely new branches of production, creating new fields of labour, are also formed, as the direct result either of machinery or of the general industrial changes brought about by it.

So long as, in a given branch of industry, the factory system extends itself at the expense of the old handicrafts or of manufacture, the result is as sure as is the result of an encounter between any army furnished with breach-loaders, and one armed with bows and arrows. This first period, during which machinery conquers its field of action, is of decisive importance owing to the extraordinary profits that it helps to produce. So soon, however, as the factory system has gained a certain breadth of footing and a definite degree of maturity, and, especially, so soon as its technical basis, machinery, is itself produced by machinery ; so soon as coal mining and iron mining, the metal industries, and the means of transport have been revolutionised ; so soon, in short, as the general conditions requisite for production by the modern industrial system have been established, this mode of production acquires an elasticity, a capacity for sudden extension by leaps and bounds that finds no hindrance except in the supply of raw material and in the disposal of the produce. On the one hand, the effect of machinery is to increase the supply of raw material. On the other hand, the cheapness of the articles produced by machinery and the improved means of transport and communication furnish the weapons for conquering foreign markets. By constantly making a part of the hands "supernumerary," modern industry, in all countries where it has taken root, gives a spur to emigration and to the colonization of foreign lands, which are thereby converted into settlements for growing the raw material of the mother country. A new and international division of labour, a division suited to the requirements of the chief centres of modern industry springs up, and converts one part of the globe into a chiefly agricultural field of production, for supplying the other part which remains a chiefly industrial field. This evolution hangs together with radical changes in agriculture which we need not here further inquire into.

The enormous power, inherent in the factory system, of expanding by jumps, and the dependence of that system on the markets of the world, necessarily beget feverish production, followed by over-filling of the markets, whereupon contraction of the markets brings on crippling of production. The life of modern industry becomes a series of periods of moderate activity, prosperity, over-production, crisis and stagnation. The uncertainty and instability to which machinery subjects the employment, and consequently the conditions of existence, of the operatives become normal, owing to these periodic changes of the industrial cycle. Except in the periods of prosperity, there rages between the capitalists the most furious combat for the share of each in the markets.

The qualitative change in mechanical industry continually discharges hands from the factory, or shuts its doors against the fresh stream of recruits, while the purely quantitative extension of the factories absorbs not only the men thrown out of work, but also fresh contingents. The workpeople are thus continually both repelled and attracted, hustled from pillar to post.

Production in all the other branches of industry not only extends, but alters its character. This is the case not only with all production on a large scale, whether employing machinery or not, but also with the so-called domestic industry, whether carried on in the houses of the workpeople or in small workshops. This modern so-called domestic industry has nothing, except the name, in common with the old-fashioned domestic industry, the existence of which presupposes independent urban handicrafts, independent peasant farming, and above all, a dwelling-house for the labourer and his family. That old-fashioned industry has now been converted into an outside department of the factory, the manufactory, or the warehouse. Besides the factory operatives, the manufacturing workmen and the handicraftsmen, whom it concentrates in large masses at one spot, and directly commands, capital also sets in motion, by means of invisible threads, another army ; that of the workers in the domestic industries, who dwell in the large towns and are also scattered over the face of the country.

Economy in the means of production, first systematically carried out in the factory system, and there, from the very beginning, coincident with the most reckless squandering of labour-power, and robbery of the conditions normally requisite for labour — this economy now shows its antagonistic and murderous side more and more in a given branch of industry, the less the social productive power of labor and the technical basis for combination of processes are developed in that branch.

So long as Factory legislation is confined to regulating the labour in factories, manufactories, &c., it is regarded as a mere interference with the exploiting rights of capital. But when it comes to regulating the so-called "home-labour," it is immediately viewed as a direct attack on the *patria potestas*, on parental authority. The tender-hearted English Parliament long affected to shrink from taking this step. The force of facts, however, compelled it at last to acknowledge that modern industry, in overturning the economical foundation on which was based the traditional family, and the family labour corresponding to it, had also unloosened all traditional family ties. The rights of the children had to be proclaimed.

The necessity for a generalization of the Factory Acts, for transforming them from an exceptional law relating to mechanical spinning and weaving — into a law affecting social production as a whole, arose from the mode in which Modern Industry was historically developed. There are two circumstances that finally turn the scale : first, the experience that capital, so soon as it finds itself subject to legal control at one point, compensates itself all the more recklessly at other points; secondly, the cry of the capitalists for equality in the conditions of competition, *i.e.*, for equal restraint on all exploitation of labour.

If the general extension of factory legislation to all trades for the purpose of protecting the working class in both mind and body has become inevitable, on the other hand that extension hastens on the general conversion of numerous isolated small industries into a few combined industries carried on upon a large scale; it therefore accelerates the concentration of capital and the exclusive predominance of the factory system. It destroys both the ancient and the transitional forms, behind which the dominion of capital is still in part concealed, and replaces them by the direct and open sway of capital; but thereby it also generalises the direct opposition to this sway. While in each individual workshop it enforces uniformity, regularity, order, and economy, it increases by the immense spur which the limitation and regulation of the working day give to technical improvement, the anarchy and the catastrophes of capitalist production as a whole, the intensity of labour, and the competition of machinery with the labourer. By the destruction of petty and domestic industries it destroys the last resort of the "redundant population," and with it the sole remaining safety-valve of the whole social mechanism. By maturing the material conditions, and the combination on a social scale of the processes of production, it matures the contradictions and antagonisms of the capitalist form of production, and thereby provides, along with the elements for the formation of a new society, the forces for exploding the old one.

In the sphere of agriculture, modern industry has a more revolutionary effect than elsewhere, for this reason, that it annihilates the peasant, that bulwark of the old society, and replaces him by the wage labourer. Thus the desire for social changes, and the class antagonisms are brought to the same level in the country as in the towns. The irrational, old-fashioned methods of agriculture are replaced by scientific ones. In agriculture as in manufacture, the transformation of production under the sway of capital means, at the same time, the martyrdom of the producer ; the instrument of labour becomes the means of enslaving, exploiting, and impoverishing the labourer ; the social combination and organisation of labour-processes is turned into an organised mode of crushing out the workman's individual vitality, freedom, and independence. The dispersion of the rural labourers over larger areas breaks their power of resistance while concentration increases that of the town operatives. In modern agriculture, as in the urban industries, the increased productiveness and quantity of the labour set in motion are bought at the cost of laying waste and consuming by disease labour-power itself. Moreover, all progress in capitalistic agriculture is a progress in the art, not only of robbing the labourer, but of robbing the soil ; all progress in increasing the fertility of the soil for a given time, is a progress towards ruining the lasting sources of that fertility. The more a country starts its development on the foundation of modern industry, like the United States, for example, the more rapid is this process of destruction. Capitalistic production, therefore, developes technology and the combining together of various processes into a social whole, only by sapping the original sources of all wealth — the soil and the labourer.

V. The Production of Absolute and of Relative Surplus-Value

14. *Absolute and Relative Surplus-Value*

As the co-operative character of the labour-process becomes more and more marked, so, as a necessary consequence, does our notion of productive labour, and of its agent the productive labourer, become extended. In order to labour productively, it is no longer necessary for you to do manual work yourself ; enough, if you are an organ of the collective labourer, and perform one of its subordinate functions. In another sense, however, our notion of productive labour becomes narrowed. That labourer alone is productive, who produces surplus-value for the capitalist, and thus works for the self-expansion of capital. Hence the notion of a productive labourer implies not merely a relation between work and useful effect, between labourer and product of labour, but also a specific, social relation of production, a relation that has sprung up historically and stamps the labourer as the direct means of creating surplus-value. In the course of this development, the formal subjection is replaced by the real subjection of labour to capital.

From one standpoint, any distinction between absolute and relative surplus-value appears illusory. Relative surplus-value is absolute, since it compels the absolute prolongation of the working day beyond the labour-time necessary to the existence of the labourer himself. Absolute surplus-value is relative, since it makes necessary such a development of the productiveness of labour, as will allow of the necessary labour-time being confined to a portion of the working day. But if we keep in mind the behaviour of surplus-value, this appearance of identity vanishes. Once the capitalist mode of production is established and becomes general, the difference between absolute and relative surplus-value makes itself felt.

Assuming that labour-power is paid for at its value, we are confronted by this alternative : given the productiveness of labour and its normal intensity, the rate of surplus-value can be raised only by the actual prolongation of the working day ; on the other hand, given the length of the working day, that rise can be effected only by a change in the relative magnitudes of the components of the working day, viz., necessary labour and surplus-labour; a change, which, if the wages are not to fall below the value of labour-power, presupposes a change either in the productiveness or in the intensity of the labour.

Thus, not only does the historically developed social productiveness of labour, but also its natural productiveness, appear to be productiveness of the capital with which that labour is incorporated.

Favourable natural conditions alone gave us only the possibility, never the reality, of surplus-labour, nor, consequently, of surplus-value and a surplus-product. The result of difference in the natural conditions of labour is this, that the same quantity of labour satisfies, in different countries, a different mass of requirements, consequently, that under circumstances in other respects analogous, the necessary labour-time is different. These conditions affect surplus-labour only as natural limits, *i.e.*, by fixing the points at which labour for others can begin. In proportion as industry advances, these natural limits recede.

15. *Changes of Magnitude in the Price of Labour-Power and in Surplus-Value*

On the assumption (1) that commodities are sold at their value; (2) that the price of labour-power rises occasionally above its value, but never sinks below it, we have seen that the relative magnitudes of surplus-value and of price of labour-power are determined by three circumstances; (1) the length of the working day, or the extensive magnitude of labour; (2) the normal intensity of labour, its intensive magnitude, whereby a given quantity of labour is expended in a given time; (3) the productiveness of labour. Very different combinations are clearly possible.

The chief combinations are: I. Length of the working day and intensity of labour constant. Productiveness of labour variable. II. Working day constant. Productiveness of labour constant. Intensity of labour

variable. III. Productiveness and intensity of labour
constant. Length of the working day variable. IV. Simultaneous variations in the duration, productiveness,
and intensity of labour.

16. *Various Formulæ for the Rate of Surplus-Value*

The rate of surplus-value is represented by the following formulæ :

$$\text{I. } \frac{\text{Surplus-value}}{\text{Variable Capital}}\left(\frac{s}{v}\right)=\frac{\text{Surplus-value}}{\text{Value of labour-power}}=\frac{\text{Surplus-labour}}{\text{Necessary labour}}$$

The first two of these formulæ represent, as a ratio of
values, that which, in the third, is represented as a ratio
of the times during which those values are produced.
These formulæ, supplementary the one to the other,
are rigorously definite and correct. In classical political
economy we meet with the following derivative formulæ :

$$\text{II. } \frac{\text{Surplus-labour}}{\text{Working day}}=\frac{\text{Surplus-value}}{\text{Value of the Product}}=\frac{\text{Surplus-product}}{\text{Total Product}}$$

One and the same ratio is here expressed as a ratio of
labour-times, of the values in which those labour-times
are embodied, and of the products in which those values
exist.

In all of these formulæ (II), the actual degree of
exploitation of labour, or the rate of surplus-value, is
falsely expressed. Let the working day be 12 hours.
Then, making the same assumptions of former instances,
the real degree of exploitation of labour will be represented in the following proportions :

$$\frac{\text{6 hours surplus-labour}}{\text{6 hours necessary labour}}=\frac{\text{Surplus-value of 3 sh.}}{\text{Variable Capital of 3 sh.}}=100\%$$

From formulæ II we get very differently,

$$\frac{\text{6 hours surplus-labour}}{\text{Working day of 12 hours}}=\frac{\text{Surplus-value of 3 sh.}}{\text{Value created of 6 sh.}}=50\%$$

These derivative formulæ express, in reality, only the
proportion in which the working day, or the value

produced by it, is divided between capitalist and labourer. If they are to be treated as direct expressions of the degree of self-expansion of capital, the following erroneous law would hold good : Surplus-labour or surplus-value can never reach 100%. Since the surplus-labour is only an aliquot part of the working day, or since surplus-value is only an aliquot part of the value created, the surplus-labour must necessarily be always less than the working day, or the surplus-value always less than the total value created. The ratio $\frac{\text{Surplus-labour}}{\text{Working day}}$ or $\frac{\text{Surplus-value}}{\text{Value created}}$ can therefore never reach the limit of $\frac{100}{100}$, still less rise to $\frac{100 + x}{100}$. But not so the rate of surplus-value, the real degree of exploitation of labour.

There is a third formula ; it is

$$\text{III.} \quad \frac{\text{Surplus-value}}{\text{Value of labour-power}} = \frac{\text{Surplus-labour}}{\text{Necessary labour}} = \frac{\text{Unpaid labour}}{\text{Paid labour}}$$

It is no longer possible to be misled, by the formula $\frac{\text{Unpaid labour}}{\text{Paid labour}}$, into concluding, that the capitalist pays for labour and not for labour-power. The capitalist pays the value of the labour-power, and receives in exchange the disposal of the living labour-power itself. Thus the capitalist receives in return for the price a product of the same price. During the period of surplus-labour, the usufruct of the labour-power creates a value for the capitalist. This expenditure of labour-power comes to him gratis. In this sense it is that surplus-labour can be called unpaid labour.

Capital, therefore, is not only, as Adam Smith says, the command over labour. It is essentially the command over unpaid labour. All surplus-value, whatever particular form (profit, interest, or rent), it may subsequently crystallise into, is in substance the materialisation of unpaid labour. The secret of the self-expansion of capital resolves itself into having the disposal of a definite quantity of other people's unpaid labour.

VI. Wages

17. The Transformation of the Value (and Respectively the Price) of Labour-Power into Wages

On the surface of bourgeois society the wage of the labourer appears as the price of labour, a certain quantity of money that is paid for a certain quantity of labour. That which comes directly face to face with the possessor of money on the market, is in fact not labour, but the labourer. What the latter sells is his labour-power. As soon as his labour actually begins, it has already ceased to belong to him ; it can therefore no longer be sold by him. Labour is the substance, and the immanent measure of value, but *has itself no value*.

The wage-form extinguishes every trace of the division of the working day into necessary labour and surplus-labour, into paid and unpaid labour. All labour appears as paid labour.

In slave-labour, even that part of the working day in which the slave is only replacing the value of his own means of existence, in which, therefore, in fact, he works for himself alone, appears as labour for his master. All the slave's labour appears as unpaid labour. In wage-labour, on the contrary, even surplus-labour, or unpaid labour, appears as paid.

Let us put ourselves in the place of the labourer who receives for 12 hours' labour, say the value produced by 6 hours' labour, say 3s. For him, in fact, his 12 hours' labour is the means of buying the 3s. The value of his labour-power may vary, with the value of his usual means of subsistence, from 3 to 4 shillings, or from 3 to 2 shillings ; or, if the value of his labour-power remains constant, its price may, in consequence of changing relations of demand and supply, rise to 4s. or fall to 2s. He always gives 12 hours of labour. Every change in the amount of the equivalent that he receives appears

to him necessarily as a change in the value or price of
his 12 hours' work.

Let us consider, on the other hand, the capitalist. He
wishes to receive as much labour as possible for as little
money as possible. Practically, therefore, the only thing
that interests him is the difference between the price
of labour-power and the value which its function creates. But, then, he tries to buy all commodities as
cheaply as possible, and always accounts for his profit
by simple cheating, by buying under, and selling over
the value. Hence, he never comes to see that, if such a
thing as the value of labour really existed and he really
paid this value, no capital would exist, his money would
not be turned into capital.

18. *Time-Wages*

The sale of labour-power takes place for a definite
period of time. The converted form under which the
daily, weekly, &c., value of labour-power presents itself, is hence that of time-wages, therefore day-wages,
&c.

The sum of money which the labourer receives for
his daily or weekly labour, forms the amount of his
nominal wages, or of his wages estimated in value. But
it is clear that according to the length of the working
day, that is, according to the amount of actual labour
daily supplied, the same daily or weekly wage may
represent very different prices of labour. We must,
therefore, in considering time-wages, again distinguish
between the sum total of the daily or weekly wages,
&c., and the price of labour. How then to find this
price, *i.e.*, the money-value of a given quantity of labour ?

The average price of labour is found, when the average daily value of the labour-power is divided by the
average number of hours in the working day. The price
of the working hour thus found serves as the unit measure for the price of labour.

The daily and weekly wages, &c., may remain the same, although the price of labour falls constantly. On the contrary, the daily or weekly wages may rise, although the price of labour remains constant or even falls. As a general law it follows that, given the amount of daily, weekly labour, &c., the daily or weekly wages depend on the price of labour, which itself varies either with the value of labour-power, or with the difference between its price and its value. Given, on the other hand, the price of labour, the daily or weekly wages depend on the quantity of the daily or weekly labour.

If the hour's wage is fixed so that the capitalist does not bind himself to pay a day's or a week's wage, but only to pay wages for the hours during which he chooses to employ the labourer, he can employ him for a shorter time than that which is originally the basis of the calculation of the hour-wage, of the unit-measure of the price of labour.

He can now wring from the labourer a certain quantity of surplus-labour without allowing him the labour-time necessary for his own subsistence. He can annihilate all regularity of employment, and according to his own convenience, caprice, and the interest of the moment, make the most enormous over-work alternate with relative or absolute cessation of work. He can, under the pretence of paying "the normal price of labour," abnormally lengthen the working day without any corresponding compensation to the labourer.

With an increasing daily or weekly wage the price of labour may remain nominally constant, and yet may fall below its normal level. This occurs every time that, the price of labour (reckoned per working hour) remaining constant, the working day is prolonged beyond its customary length. It is a fact generally known that, the longer the working days, in any branch of industry, the lower are the wages.

The same circumstances which allow the capitalist

in the long run to prolong the working day, also allow him first, and compel him finally, nominally to lower the price of labour until the total price of the increased number of hours is lowered, and, therefore, the daily or weekly wage.

This command over abnormal quantities of unpaid labour, *i.e.*, quantities in excess of the average social amount, becomes a source of competition amongst the capitalists themselves. A part of the price of the commodity consists of the price of labour.

19. *Piece-Wages*

Wages by the piece are nothing else than a converted form of wages by time. In time-wages the labour is measured by its immediate duration, in piece-wages by the quantity of products in which the labour has embodied itself during a given time. It is not, therefore, a question of measuring the value of the piece by the working time incorporated in it, but on the contrary of measuring the working time the labourer has expended, by the number of pieces he has produced.

Piece-wages furnish to the capitalist an exact measure for the intensity of labour. Only the working time which is embodied in a quantum of commodities determined beforehand and experimentally fixed counts as socially necessary working time, and is paid as such. The quality of the labour is here controlled by the work itself, which must be of average perfection if the piece-price is to be paid in full. Piece-wages become, from this point of view, the most fruitful source of reductions of wages and capitalistic cheating.

Since the quality and intensity of the work are here controlled by the form of wage itself, superintendence of labour becomes in great part superfluous. Piece-wages therefore lay the foundation of the modern "domestic labour," as well as of a hierarchically organised system of exploitation and oppression. The latter has two fundamental forms : the interposition of parasites between the capitalist and the wage-labourer, and the "sub-letting of labour."

The exploitation of the labourer by capital is here effected through the exploitation of the labourer by the labourer.

In time-wages, with few exceptions, the same wage holds for the same kind of work, whilst in piece-wages, though the price of the working time is measured by a certain quantity of product, the day's or week's wage will vary with the individual differences of the labourers, of whom one supplies in a given time the minimum of product only, another the average, a third more than the average. With regard to actual receipts there is, therefore, great variety according to the different skill, strength, energy, staying-power, etc., of the individual labourers.

Of course this does not alter the general relations between capital and wage-labour. First, the individual differences balance one another in the workshop as a whole, which thus supplies in a given working-time the average product, and the total wages paid will be the average wages of that particular branch of industry. Second, the proportion between wages and surplus-value remains unaltered, since the mass of surplus-labour supplied by each particular labourer corresponds with the wage received by him. But the wider scope that piece-wage gives to individuality tends to develop on the one hand that individuality, and with it the sense of liberty, independence, and self-control of the labourers, on the other, their competition one with another. Piece-work has, therefore, a tendency, while raising individual wages above the average, to lower this average itself.

Piece-wage is the form of wages most in harmony with the capitalist mode of production. It only conquers a larger field for action during the period of Manufacture, properly so-called. In the stormy youth

of Modern Industry, it served as a lever for the lengthening of the working day, and the lowering of wages.
In the workshops under the Factory Acts, piece-wage
becomes the general rule, because capital can there only
increase the efficacy of the working day by intensify-
ing labour.

20. *National Differences of Wages*

In every country there is a certain average intensity
of labour, below which the labour for the production
of a commodity requires more than the socially necessary time, and therefore does not reckon as labour of
normal quality. Only a degree of intensity above the
national average affects, in a given country, the measure of value of the mere duration of the working time.
This is not the case on the universal market, whose in-
tegral parts are the individual countries. The average
intensity of labour changes from country to country ;
here it is greater, there less. These national averages
form a scale, whose unit of measure is the average unit
of universal labour. The more intense national labour,
therefore, as compared with the less intense, produces
in the same time more value, which expresses itself in
more money.

The relative value of money will be less in the nation
with more developed capitalist mode of production
than in the nation with less developed. It follows, then,
that the nominal wages, the equivalent of labour-power
expressed in money, will also be higher in the first nation
than in the second ; which does not at all prove that this
holds also for the real wages, *i.e.*, for the means of subsistence placed at the disposal of the labourer.

VII. The Accumulation of Capital

The conversion of a sum of money into means of
production and labour-power is the first step taken by
the quantum of value that is going to function as capi-

tal. This conversion takes place in the market, within the sphere of circulation. The second step, the process of production, is complete so soon as the means of production have been converted into commodities whose value exceeds that of their component parts, and, therefore, contains the capital originally advanced, plus a surplus-value. These commodities must then be thrown into circulation. They must be sold, their value realised in money, this money afresh converted into capital, and so over and over again. This movement forms the circulation of capital.

21. *Simple Reproduction*

A society can no more cease to produce than it can cease to consume. Therefore, every social process of production is, at the same time, a process of reproduction.

The conditions of production are also those of reproduction. If production be capitalistic in form, so, too, will be reproduction. Just as in the former the labour-process figures but as a means towards the self-expansion of capital, so in the latter it figures but as a means of reproducing as capital the value advanced. It is only because his money constantly functions as capital that the economical guise of a capitalist attaches to a man.

Simple reproduction is a mere repetition of the process of production on the old scale.

As a periodic increment of the capital advanced, or periodic fruit of capital in process, surplus-value acquires the form of a revenue flowing out of capital.

The value of the capital advanced divided by the surplus-value annually consumed, gives the number of years, or reproduction periods, at the expiration of which the capital originally advanced has been consumed by the capitalist and has disappeared. After the lapse of a certain number of years the capital value he then possesses is equal to the sum total of the surplus-value appropriated by him during those years, and the total value he has consumed is equal to that of his original capital.

The mere continuity of the process of production, in other words simple reproduction, sooner or later, and of necessity, converts every capital into accumulated capital, or capitalised surplus-value. If that capital was originally acquired by the personal labour of its employer, it sooner or later becomes value appropriated without an equivalent, the unpaid labour of others materialised either in money or in some other object.

That which at first was but a starting point, becomes, by the mere continuity of the process, by simple reproduction, the peculiar result, constantly renewed and perpetuated, of capitalist production. On the one hand, the process of production incessantly converts material wealth into capital, into means of creating more wealth and means of enjoyment for the capitalist. On the other hand the labourer, on quitting the process, is what he was on entering it, a source of wealth, but devoid of all means of making that wealth his own. The labourer constantly produces material, objective wealth, but in the form of capital, of an alien power that dominates and exploits him; and the capitalist as constantly produces labour-power, but in the form of a subjective source of wealth, separated from the objects in and by which it can alone be realised; in short he produces the labourer, but as a wage-labourer.

The labourer consumes in a twofold way. While producing he consumes by his labour the means of production, and converts them into products with a higher value than that of the capital advanced. This is his productive consumption. On the other hand, the labourer turns the money paid to him for his labour-power, into means of subsistence : this is his individual consumption. Productive consumption and individual consumption are totally distinct. In the former, he acts as the motive power of capital, and belongs to the capitalist. In the latter, he belongs to himself, and performs his necessary vital functions outside the process of production. The result of the one is, that the capitalist lives ; of the other, that the labourer lives.

By converting part of his capital into labour-power, the capitalist augments the value of his entire capital. He kills two birds with one stone. He profits, not only by what he receives from, but by what he gives to, the labourer. The capital is converted into necessaries, by the consumption of which the muscles, nerves, bones, and brains of existing labourers are reproduced, and new labourers are begotten.

The individual consumption of the working class is, therefore, the production and reproduction of that means of production so indispensable to the capitalist : the labourer himself. The maintenance and reproduction of the working class is, and must ever be, a necessary condition to the reproduction of capital.

Hence the capitalist considers that part alone of the labourer's individual consumption to be productive, which is requisite for the perpetuation of the class ; what the labourer consumes for his own pleasure beyond that part, is unproductive consumption. In reality, the individual consumption of the labourer is unproductive as regards himself, for it reproduces nothing but the needy individual ; it is productive to the capitalist and the State, since it is the production of the power that creates their wealth.

From a social point of view, therefore, the working class, even when not directly engaged in the labour-process, is just as much an appendage of capital as the ordinary instruments of labour. Even its individual consumption is, within certain limits, a mere factor in the process of production. The Roman slave was held by fetters : the wage-labourer is bound to his owner by invisible threads. The reproduction of the working class carries with it the accumulation of skill, that is handed down from one generation to another.

Capitalist production reproduces the separation between labour-power and the means of labour. It thereby reproduces and perpetuates the condition for exploiting. It incessantly forces him to sell his labour-power in order to live, and enables the capitalist to purchase labour-power in order that he may enrich himself. It is no longer a mere accident, that capitalist and labourer confront each other in the market as buyer and seller. It is the process itself that incessantly hurls back the labourer on to the market as a vendor of his labour-power, and that incessantly converts his own product into a means by which another man can purchase him. In reality, the labourer belongs to capital before he has sold himself to capital. His economical bondage is both brought about and concealed by the periodic sale of himself, by his change of masters, and by the oscillations in the market price of labour-power.

Capitalist production, therefore, under its aspect of a continuous connected process, of a process of reproduction, produces not only commodities, not only surplus-value, but it also produces and reproduces the capitalist relation.

22. *Conversion of Surplus-Value into Capital*

Employing surplus-value as capital, reconverting it into capital, is called accumulation of capital.

To accumulate, it is necessary to convert a portion of the surplus-product into capital. But we cannot, except by a miracle, convert into capital anything but such articles as can be employed in the labour-process (*i.e.*, means of production), and means of subsistence. Consequently, a part of the annual surplus-labour must have been applied to the production of additional means of production and subsistence, over and above the quantity of these things required to replace the capital advanced. In one word, surplus-value is convertible into capital solely because the surplus-product, whose value it is, already comprises the material elements of new capital.

In order to allow of these elements actually functioning, the capitalist class requires additional labour. If the
exploitation of the labourers already employed should
not increase, either extensively or intensively, then additional labour-power must be found. For this the mechanism of capitalist production provides beforehand, by
converting the working class into a class dependent on
wages, a class whose ordinary wages suffice, not only
for its maintenance, but for its increase. It is only necessary for capital to incorporate this additional labour-
power, with the surplus means of production, and the
conversion of surplus-value into capital is complete.

It is the old story : Abraham begat Isaac, Isaac begat
Jacob, and so on. The original capital of £10,000 brings
in a surplus-value of £2000, which is capitalised. The
new capital of £2000 brings in a surplus-value of £400,
and this, too, is capitalised, converted into a second additional capital, and, in its turn, produces a further
surplus-value of £80. And so the ball rolls on.

At first the rights of property seemed to us to be
based on a man's own labour. At least, some such assumption was necessary since only commodity owners
with equal rights confronted each other, and the sole
means by which a man could become possessed of the
commodities of others, was by alienating his own commodities ; and these could be replaced by labour alone.
Now, however, property turns out to be the right, on
the part of the capitalist, to appropriate the unpaid labour of others or its product and to be the impossibility,
on the part of the labourer, of appropriating his own
product. The separation of property from labour has
become the necessary consequence of a law that apparently originated in their identity.

We have seen that even in the case of simple reproduction, all capital, whatever its original source, becomes converted into accumulated capital, capitalised
surplus-value. But in the flood of production all the
capital originally advanced becomes a vanishing quan-

tity (*magnitudo evanescens*, in the mathematical sense), compared with the directly accumulated capital, *i.e.*, with the surplus-value or surplus product that is reconverted into capital, whether it function in the hands of its accumulator, or in those of others.

One portion is consumed by the capitalist as revenue, the other is employed as capital, is accumulated. Given the mass of surplus-value, then, the larger the one of these parts, the smaller is the other. The ratio of these parts determines the magnitude of the accumulation. But it is by the owner of the surplus-value, by the capitalist alone, that the division is made. It is his deliberate act. Except as personified capital, the capitalist has no historical value, and no right to existence.

Only as personified capital is the capitalist respectable. As such, he shares with the miser the passion for wealth as wealth. Fanatically bent on making value expand itself, he ruthlessly forces the human race to produce for production's sake ; he thus forces the development of the productive powers of society, and creates those material conditions, which alone can form the real basis of a higher form of society. To accumulate is to conquer the world of social wealth, to increase the mass of human beings exploited by him, and thus to extend both the direct and the indirect sway of the capitalist.

At the historical dawn of capitalist production — and every capitalist upstart has personally to go through this historical stage — avarice, and desire to get rich, are the ruling passions. But the progress not only creates a world of delights ; it lays open, in speculation and the credit system, a thousand sources of sudden enrichment. When a certain stage of development has been reached, a conventional degree of prodigality, which is also an exhibition of wealth, and consequently a source of credit, becomes a business necessity to the "unfortunate" capitalist. Luxury enters into capital's expenses of representation. Although, therefore, the prodigality of the capitalist never possesses the bona-fide character of the open-handed feudal lord's prodigality, but, on the contrary, has always lurking behind it the most sordid avarice and the most anxious calculation, yet his expenditure grows with his accumulation.

Circumstances that, independently of the division of surplus-value into capital and revenue, determine the amount of accumulation are : degree of exploitation of labour-power ; productivity of labour ; growing difference in amount between capital employed and capital consumed ; magnitude of capital advanced. By incorporating with itself the two primary creators of wealth, labour-power and the land, capital acquires a power of expansion that permits it to augment the elements of its accumulation beyond the limits apparently fixed by its own magnitude, or by the value and the mass of the means of production, already produced, in which it has its being.

An important factor in the accumulation of capital is the degree of productivity of social labour. The development of the productive power of labour reacts also on the original capital already engaged in the process of production. The old capital is reproduced in a more productive form. Every introduction of improved methods works almost simultaneously on the new capital and on that already in action. Every advance in Chemistry not only multiplies the number of useful materials and the useful applications of those already known, thus extending with the growth of capital its sphere of investment. It teaches at the same time how to throw the excrements of the processes of production and consumption back again into the circle of the process of reproduction, and thus, without any previous outlay of capital, creates new matter for capital. Like the increased exploitation of natural wealth by the mere increase in the tension of labour-power, science and technology give capital a power of expansion independent of the given magnitude of the capital actually functioning. They react at the same time on that part of the original capital which has entered upon its stage of renewal. This, in passing into its new shape, incorporates gratis the social advance made while its old shape was being used up. Hence, with the increase in efficacy, extent and value of its means of production, labour keeps up and eternises an always increasing capital-value in a form ever new. This natural power of labour takes the appearance of an intrinsic property of capital.

23. The General Law of Capitalist Accumulation

The composition of capital is to be understood in a twofold sense. On the side of value, it is determined by the proportion in which it is divided into constant and variable capital. On the side of material, as it functions in the process of production, all capital is divided into means of production and living labour-power. I call the former the *value-composition*, the latter the *technical composition* of capital. Between the two there is a strict correlation. I call the value-composition of capital, in so far as it is determined by its technical composition and mirrors the changes of the latter, the *organic composition* of capital.

The many individual capitals invested in a particular branch of production have, one with another, more or less different compositions. The average of their individual compositions gives the composition of the total capital in this branch of production. Lastly, the average of these averages, in all branches of production, gives the composition of the total social capital of a country, and with this alone are we concerned in the following investigation.

Growth of capital involves growth of its variable constituent. A part of the surplus-value turned into additional capital must always be retransformed into variable capital, or additional labour-fund. If we suppose that a definite mass of means of production constantly needs the same mass of labour-power then the demand for labour and the subsistence-fund of the labourers clearly increase in the same proportion as the capital, and the more rapidly, the more rapidly the capital increases. The requirements of accumulating capital may exceed the increase of labour-power or of the number of labourers ; the demand for labourers may exceed the supply and, therefore, wages may rise.

As simple reproduction constantly reproduces the capital-relation itself, *i.e.*, the relation of capitalists on the one hand, and wage-workers on the other, so reproduction on a progressive scale, *i.e.*, accumulation, reproduces the capital-relation on a progressive scale, more capitalists or larger capitalists at this pole, more wage-workers at that. The reproduction of a mass of labour-power, which must incessantly re-incorporate itself with capital for that capital's self-expansion ; which cannot get free from capital, and whose enslavement to capital is only concealed by the variety of individual capitalists to whom it sells itself, this reproduction of labour-power forms, in fact, an essential of the reproduction of capital itself. Accumulation of capital is, therefore, increase of the proletariat.

Under the conditions of accumulation, which conditions are those most favourable to the labourers, their relation of dependence upon capital takes on a form endurable. A larger part of their own surplus-product, always increasing and continually transformed into additional capital, comes back to them in the shape of means of payment, so that they can extend the circle of their enjoyments ; can make some additions to their consumption-fund of clothes, furniture, &c., and can lay by small reserve-funds of money. But just as little as better clothing, food, and treatment, and a larger peculium, do away with the exploitation of the slave, so little do they set aside that of the wage-worker. A rise in the price of labour, as a consequence of accumulation of capital, only means, in fact, that the length and weight of the golden chain the wage-worker has already forged for himself, allow of a relaxation of the tension of it.

With the use of machinery, a greater mass of raw material and auxiliary substances enter into the labour-process. That is the consequence of the increasing productivity of labour. On the other hand, the mass of machinery, beasts of burden, mineral manures, drain-pipes, &c., is a condition of the increasing productivity of labour. So also is it with the means of production concentrated in buildings, furnaces, means of transport, &c. But whether condition or consequence, the growing extent of the means of production, as compared with the labour-power incorporated with them, is an expression of the growing productiveness of labour. The increase of the latter appears in the diminution of the mass of labour in proportion to the mass of means of production moved by it, or in the diminution of the subjective factor of the labour process as compared with the objective factor.

This change in the technical composition of capital, this growth in the mass of means of production, as compared with the mass of the labour-power that vivifies them, is reflected again in its value-composition, by the increase of the constant constituent of capital at the expense of its variable constituent. This law of the progressive increase in constant capital, in proportion to the variable, is confirmed at every step by the comparative analysis of the prices of commodities, whether we compare different economic epochs or different nations in the same epoch. The relative magnitude of the element of price, which represents the value of the means of production only, or the constant part of capital consumed, is in direct, the relative magnitude of the other element of price that pays labour (the variable part of capital) is in inverse proportion to the advance of accumulation.

This diminution in the variable part of capital as compared with the constant, or the altered value-composition of the capital, however, only shows approximately the change in the composition of its material constituents. With the increasing productivity of labour, not only does the mass of the means of production consumed by it increase, but their value compared with their mass diminishes. Their value therefore rises absolutely, but not in proportion to their mass. The increase of the difference between constant and variable capital is, therefore, much less than that of the difference between the mass of the means of production into which the constant, and the mass of the labour-power into which the variable, capital is converted. The former difference increases with the latter, but in a smaller degree. But, if the progress of accumulation lessens the relative magnitude of the variable part of capital, it by no means, in doing this, excludes the possibility of a rise in its absolute magnitude.

Every individual capital is a larger or smaller concentration of means of production, with a corresponding command over a larger or smaller labour-army. Every accumulation becomes the means of new accumulation. Accumulation increases the concentration of that wealth in the hands of individual capitalists, and thereby widens the basis of production on a large scale and of the specific methods of capitalist production. The growth of social capital is effected by the growth of many individual capitals. All other circumstances remaining the same, individual capitals, and with them the concentration of the means of production, increases in such proportion as they form aliquot parts of the total social capital.

Accumulation, therefore, presents itself on the one hand as increasing concentration of the means of production, and of the command over labour ; on the other, as repulsion of many individual capitals one from another. This splitting-up of the total social capital into many individual capitals or the repulsion of its fractions one from another, is counteracted by their attraction. This last does not mean simple concentration, which is identical with accumulation. It is concentration of capitals already formed, destruction of their individual independence, expropriation of capitalist by capitalist, transformation of many small into few large capitals. This process differs from the former in this, that it only presupposes a change in the distribution of capital already to hand, and functioning; its field of action is therefore not limited by the absolute growth of social wealth, by the absolute limits of accumulation. Capital grows in one place to a huge mass in a single hand, because it has in another place been lost by many. This is centralisation proper, as distinct from accumulation and concentration.

Centralisation supplements the work of accumulation, by enabling the industrial capitalists to expand the scale of their operations. Whether centralisation is accomplished by the violent means of annexation, or whether it proceeds by the smoother road of forming stock companies, the economic result remains the same : progressive transformation of isolated processes of production carried on in accustomed ways into socially combined and scientifically managed processes of production.

The masses of capital amalgamated over night by centralisation reproduce and augment themselves like the others, only faster, and thus become new and powerful levers of social accumulation. The additional capitals serve mainly as vehicles for the exploitation of new inventions and discoveries, or of industrial improvements in general. However, the old capital likewise arrives in due time at the moment when it must renew its head and limbs, when it casts off its old skin and is likewise born again in its perfected industrial form, in which a smaller quantity of labor suffices to set in motion a larger quantity of machinery and raw materials. The absolute decrease of the demand for labor necessarily following therefrom will naturally be so much greater, the more these capitals going through the process of rejuvenation have become accumulated in masses by means of the movement of centralisation.

The labouring population produces, along with the accumulation of capital, the means by which itself is made relatively superfluous ; and it does this to an always increasing extent. This is a law of population peculiar to the capitalist mode of production.

But if a surplus labouring population is a necessary product of accumulation or of the development of wealth on a capitalist basis, this surplus population becomes, conversely, the lever of capitalistic accumulation, nay, a condition of existence of the capitalist mode of production. It forms a disposable industrial reserve army, that belongs to capital quite as absolutely as if the latter had bred it at its own cost. Independently of the limits of the actual increase of population, it creates, for the changing needs of the self-expansion of capital, a mass of human material always ready for exploitation.

The course characteristic of modern industry, viz., a decennial cycle (interrupted by smaller oscillations), of periods of average activity, production at high pressure, crisis and stagnation, depends on the constant formation, the greater or less absorption, and the reformation of the industrial reserve army of surplus population. In their turn, the varying phases of the industrial cycle recruit the surplus population, and become one of the most energetic agents of its reproduction. The whole form of the movement of modern industry depends upon the constant transformation of a part of the labouring population into unemployed or half-employed hands.

The setting free of labourers goes on yet more rapidly than the technical revolution of the process of production that accompanies, and is accelerated by, the advances of accumulation ; and more rapidly than the corresponding diminution of the variable part of capital as compared with the constant. If the means of production, as they increase in extent and effective power, become to a less extent means of employment of labourers, this state of things is again modified by the fact that in proportion as the productiveness of labour increases, capital increases its supply of labour more quickly than its demand for labourers. The over-work of the employed part of the working class swells the ranks of the reserve, whilst conversely the greater pressure that the latter by its competition exerts on the former, forces these to submit to over-work and to subjugation under the dictates of capital. The condemnation of one part of the working class to enforced idleness by the over-work of the other part, and the converse, becomes a means of enriching the individual capitalists, and accelerates at the same time the production of the industrial reserve army on a scale corresponding with the advance of social accumulation.

Taking them as a whole, the general movements of wages are exclusively regulated by the expansion and contraction of the industrial reserve army, and these again correspond to the periodic changes of the industrial cycle. They are, therefore, not determined by the variations of the absolute number of the working population, but by the varying proportions in which the working class is divided into active and reserve army, by the increase and diminution in the relative amount of the surplus-population, by the extent to which it is now absorbed, now set free.

The industrial reserve army, during the periods of stagnation and average prosperity, weighs down the active labour-army ; during the periods of over-production and paroxysm, it holds its pretensions in check. Relative surplus-population is therefore the pivot upon which the law of demand and supply of labour works. It confines the field of action of this law within the

limits absolutely convenient to the activity of exploitation and to the domination of capital, and completes
the despotism of capital.

The relative surplus population exists in every possible form. Every labourer belongs to it during the
time when he is only partially employed or wholly unemployed. Not taking into account the great periodi-
cally recurring forms that the changing phases of the
industrial cycle impress on it, now an acute form during
the crisis, then again a chronic form during dull times —
it has always three forms, the floating, the latent, the
stagnant.

The consumption of labour-power by capital is, besides, so rapid that the labourer, half-way through his
life, has already more or less completely lived himself
out. It is precisely among the workpeople of modern
industry that we meet with the shortest duration of life.
Hence, rapid renewal of the generations of labourers.

Not only the number of births and deaths, but the
absolute size of the families stand in inverse proportion
to the height of wages, and therefore to the amount of
means of subsistence of which the different categories
of labourers dispose. This law of capitalistic society
would sound absurd to savages. It calls to mind the
boundless reproduction of animals individually weak
and constantly hunted down.

As soon as capitalist production takes possession of
agriculture, and in proportion to the extent to which it
does so, the demand for an agricultural labouring population falls absolutely, while the accumulation of the
capital employed in agriculture advances, without this
repulsion being, as in nonagricultural industries, compensated by a greater attraction. Part of the agricultural population is therefore constantly on the point of
passing over into an urban or manufacturing proletariat.
This source of relative surplus-population is constantly
flowing. But the constant flow towards the towns presupposes, in the country itself, a constant latent surplus-

population. The agricultural labourer is therefore reduced to the minimum of wages, and always stands with one foot already in the swamp of pauperism.

The lowest sediment of the relative surplus-population finally dwells in the sphere of pauperism. Exclusive of vagabonds, criminals, prostitutes, in a word, the "dangerous" classes, this layer of society consists of three categories. First, those able to work. Second, orphans and pauper children. Third, the demoralized and ragged, those unable to work, the mutilated, the sickly, the widows, &c. Pauperism is the hospital of the active labour-army and the dead weight of the industrial reserve-army.

The greater the social wealth, the functioning capital, the extent and energy of its growth, and, therefore, also the absolute mass of the proletariat and the productiveness of its labour, the greater is the industrial reserve-army. The same causes which develope the expansive power of capital, developes also the labour-power at its disposal. The relative mass of the industrial reserve-army increases therefore with the potential energy of wealth. But the greater this reserve-army in proportion to the active labour-army, the greater is the mass of a consolidated surplus-population, whose misery is in inverse ratio to its torment of labour. The more extensive, finally, the lazarus-layers of the working-class, and the industrial reserve-army, the greater is official pauperism. *This is the absolute general law of capitalist accumulation.*

It follows therefore that in proportion as capital accumulates, the lot of the labourer, be his payment high or low, must grow worse. The law, finally, that always equilibrates the relative surplus-population, or industrial reserve army, to the extent and energy of accumulation, this law rivets the labourer to capital more firmly than the wedges of Vulcan did Prometheus to the rock. It establishes an accumulation of misery, corresponding with accumulation of capital. Accumulation of wealth at one pole is, therefore, at the same time accumulation of misery, agony of toil, slavery, ignorance, brutality, mental degradation, at the opposite pole.

24. *The So-Called Primitive Accumulation*

We have seen how money is changed into capital; how through capital surplus-value is made, and from surplus-value more capital. But the accumulation of capital presupposes surplus-value; surplus-value presupposes capitalistic production; capitalistic production presupposes the pre-existence of considerable masses of capital and of labour-power in the hands of producers of commodities. The whole movement, therefore, seems to turn in a vicious circle, out of which we can only escape by supposing a primitive accumulation preceding capitalistic accumulation; an accumulation not the result of the capitalist mode of production, but its starting point. This primitive accumulation plays in Political Economy about the same part as original sin in theology. Adam bit the apple, and thereupon sin fell on the human race.

The process, that clears the way for the capitalist system, can be none other than the process which takes away from the labourer the possession of his means of production; a process that transforms, on the one hand, the social means of subsistence and of production into capital, on the other, the immediate producers into wage-labourers. The so-called primitive accumulation, therefore, is nothing else than the historical process of divorcing the producer from the means of production. It appears as primitive, because it forms the pre-historic stage of capital and of the mode of production corresponding with it.

The economic structure of capitalistic society has grown out of the economic structure of feudal society. The dissolution of the latter set free the elements of the former. The immediate producer, the labourer, could only dispose of his own person after he had ceased to be attached to the soil and ceased to be the slave, serf, or bondman of another. To become a free seller of labour-power, who carries his commodity wherever he finds a market, he must further have escaped from the regime of the guilds, their rules for apprentices and journeymen, and the impediments of their labour regulations. Hence, the historical movement which changes the producers into wage-workers, appears, on the one hand, as their emancipation from serfdom and from the fetters of the guilds, and this side alone exists for our bourgeois historians. But, on the other hand, these new freedmen became sellers of themselves only after they had been robbed of all their own means of production, and of all the guarantees of existence afforded by the old feudal arrangements. And the history of this, their expropriation, is written in the annals of mankind in letters of blood and fire.

The industrial capitalists, these new potentates, had on their part not only to displace the guild masters of handicrafts, but also the feudal lords, the possessors of the sources of wealth. In this respect their conquest of social power appears as the fruit of a victorious struggle both against feudal lordship and its revolting prerogatives, and against the guilds and the fetters they laid on the free development of production and the free exploitation of man by man. The chevaliers d'industrie, however, only succeed in supplanting the chevaliers of the sword by making use of events of which they themselves were wholly innocent.

The starting-point of the development that gave rise to the wage-labourer as well as to the capitalist, was the servitude of the labourer. The advance consisted in a change of form of this servitude, in the transformation of feudal exploitation into capitalist exploitation. To understand its march, we need not go back very far. Although we come across the first beginnings of capitalist production as early as the 14th or 15th century, sporadically, in certain towns of the Mediterranean, the capitalistic era dates from the 16th century.

In the history of primitive accumulation, all revolutions are epoch-making that act as levers for the capitalist class in course of formation ; but, above all, those moments when great masses of men are suddenly and forcibly torn from their means of subsistence, and hurled as free and "unattached" proletarians on the labour market. The expropriation of the agricultural producer, of the peasant, from the soil, is the basis of the whole process. The history of this expropriation, in different countries, assumes different aspects, and runs through its various phases in different orders of succession, and at different periods. In England alone has it the classic form.

The prelude of the revolution that laid the foundation of the capitalist mode of production was played in the last third of the 15th, and the first decade of the 16th century. A mass of free proletarians was hurled on the labour-market by the breaking-up of the bands of feudal retainers. The great feudal lords created an incomparably larger proletariat by the forcible driving of the peasantry from the land, to which the latter had the same feudal right as the lord himself, and by the usurpation of the common lands. The rapid rise of the Flemish wool manufactures, and the corresponding rise in the price of wool in England, gave the direct impulse to these evictions. Transformation of arable land into sheep-walks was, therefore, the cry.

The process of forcible expropriation of the people received in the 16th century a new and frightful impulse from the Reformation, and from the consequent colossal spoliation of the church property. The property of the church formed the religious bulwark of the traditional conditions of landed property. With its fall these were no longer tenable.

After the restoration of the Stuarts, the landed proprietors carried, by legal means, an act of usurpation, effected everywhere on the Continent without any legal formality. They abolished the feudal tenure of land, *i.e.*, they got rid of all its obligations to the State, "indemnified" the State by taxes on the peasantry and the rest of the mass of the people, vindicated for themselves the rights of modern private property in estates to which they had only a feudal title, and, finally, passed those laws of settlement, which had the same effect on the English agricultural labourer, as the edict of the Tartar Boris Godunof on the Russian peasantry.

The "glorious Revolution" brought into power, along with William of Orange, the landlord and capitalist appropriators of surplus-value. They inaugurated the new era by practising on a colossal scale thefts of state lands, thefts that had been hitherto managed more modestly. These estates were given away, sold at a ridiculous figure, or even annexed to private estates by direct seizure. All this happened without the slightest observation of legal etiquette. The crown lands thus fraudulently appropriated form the basis of the today princely domains of the English oligarchy.

The last process of wholesale expropriation of the agricultural population from the soil is, finally, the so-called clearing of estates, *i.e.*, the sweeping men off them. All the English methods hitherto considered culminated in "clearing." In Scotland areas as large as German principalities were dealt with. Part of the sheep-walks were turned into deer preserves.

The spoliation of the church's property, the fraudulent alienation of the State domains, the robbery of the common lands, the usurpation of feudal and clan property, and its transformation into modern private property under circumstances of reckless terrorism, were just so many idyllic methods of primitive accumulation. They conquered the field for capitalistic agriculture, made the soil part and parcel of capital, and created for the town industries the necessary supply of a "free" and outlawed proletariat.

The proletariat created by the breaking up of the bands of feudal retainers and by the forcible expropriation of the people from the soil, this "free" proletariat could not possibly be absorbed by the nascent manufactures as fast as it was thrown upon the world. On the other hand, these men, suddenly dragged from their wonted mode of life, could not as suddenly adapt themselves to the discipline of their new condition. They were turned *en masse* into beggars, robbers, vagabonds, partly from inclination, in most cases from stress of circumstances. Hence at the end of the 15th and during the whole of the 16th century, throughout Western Europe a bloody legislation against vagabondage. Legislation treated them as "voluntary" criminals, and assumed that it depended on their own goodwill to go on working under the old conditions that no longer existed. Thus were the agricultural people, first forcibly expropriated from the soil, driven from their homes, turned into vagabonds, and then whipped, branded, tortured by laws grotesquely terrible, into the discipline necessary for the wage system.

The class of wage-labourers formed then and in the following century only a very small part of the population, well protected in its position by the independent peasant proprietary in the country and the guild-organisation in the town. Variable capital preponderated greatly over constant. The demand for wage-labour grew, therefore, rapidly with every accumulation of capital, whilst the supply of wage-labour followed but slowly. A large part of the national product, changed later into a fund of capitalist accumulation, then still entered into the consumption fund of the labourer. Legislation on wage-labour (from the first, aimed at the exploitation of the labourer and, as it advanced, always equally hostile to him) is started in England by the Statute of Labourers, of Edward III, 1349. The ordinance of 1350 in France, issued in the name of King John, corresponds with it.

It was forbidden, under pain of imprisonment, to pay higher wages than those fixed by the statute, but the taking of higher wages was more severely punished than the giving them. A statute of 1360 increased the penalties. Coalition of the labourers is treated as a heinous crime from the 14th century to 1825. The barbarous laws against Trades' Unions fell in 1825 before the threatening bearing of the proletariat. Despite this, they fell only in part. Certain beautiful fragments of the old statute vanished only in 1859. During the very first storms of the revolution, the French bourgeoisie dared to take away from the workers the right of association but just acquired. By a decree of June 14, 1791, they declared all coalition of the workers as "an attempt against liberty and the declaration of the rights of man," punishable by a fine of 500 livres, together with deprivation of the rights of an active citizen for one year. This law which, by means of State compulsion, confined the struggle between capital and labour within limits comfortable for capital, has outlived revolutions and changes of dynasties. Even the Reign of Terror left it untouched.

As far as concerns the genesis of the farmer, we can, so to say, put our hand on it, because it is a slow process evolving through many centuries. In England the first form of the farmer is the bailiff, himself a serf. His position is similar to that of the old Roman *villicus*. Soon he becomes a half-farmer, advances one part of the agricultural stock, the landlord the other. The two divide the total product in proportions determined by contract. This form quickly disappears in England, to give place to the farmer proper, who makes his own capital breed by employing wage-labourers, and pays a part of the surplus product, in money or in kind, to the landlord as rent. To this, was added in the 16th century, a very important element. The continuous rise in the price of all agricultural produce swelled the money capital of the farmer without any action on his part, whilst the rent he paid (being calculated on the old value of money) diminished in reality. Thus they grew rich at the expense of both their labourers and their landlords.

The expropriation and eviction of a part of the agricultural population not only set free for industrial capital the labourers, their means of subsistence, and material for labour ; it also created the home market.

Formerly, the peasant family produced the means of subsistence and the raw materials, which they themselves, for the most part, consumed. These raw materials and means of subsistence have now become commodities. The many scattered customers, whom stray artisans until now had found in the numerous small producers working on their own account, concentrate themselves now into one great market provided for by industrial capital. Thus, hand in hand with the expropriation of the self-supporting peasants, with their separation from their means of production, goes the destruction of rural domestic industry, the process of separation between manufacture and agriculture.

The genesis of the industrial capitalist did not proceed in such a way as that of the farmer. Doubtless many small guild-masters, and yet more independent small artisans, or even wage-labourers, transformed themselves into small capitalists, and (by extending exploitation of wage-labour and corresponding accumulation) into full-blown capitalists. The snail's-pace of this method corresponded in no wise with the commercial requirements of the new world-market that the great discoveries of the end of the 15th century created. The Middle Age had handed down two distinct forms of capital, which mature in the most different economic social formations, usurer's capital and merchant's capital. The money capital was prevented from turning into industrial capital, in the country by the feudal constitution, in the towns by the guild organisation. These fetters vanished with the dissolution of feudal society, with the expropriation and partial eviction of the country population. The new manufacturers were established at seaports, or in inland points beyond the control of the old municipalities and their guilds.

The discovery of gold and silver in America, the extirpation, enslavement, and entombment in mines of the aboriginal population, the beginning of the conquest and looting of the East Indies, the turning of Africa into a warren for the commercial hunting of black-skins, signalised the rosy dawn of the era of capitalist production. These idyllic proceedings are the chief momenta of primitive accumulation. On their heels treads the commercial war of the European nations, with the globe for a theatre. It begins with the revolt of the Netherlands from Spain, assumes giant dimensions in England's anti-jacobin war, and is still going on in the opium wars against China, &c. The different momenta of primitive accumulation distribute themselves now, more or less in chronological order, particularly over Spain, Portugal, Holland, France, and England. In England at the end of the 17th century, they arrive at a systematical combination, embracing the colonies, the national debt, the modern mode of taxation, and the protectionist system.

These methods depend in part on brute force, e.g., the colonial system. But they all employ the power of the State, the concentrated and organised force of society, to hasten, hothouse fashion, the process of transformation of the feudal mode of production into the capitalist mode, and to shorten the transition. Force is the midwife of every old society pregnant with a new one. It is itself an economic power.

Of the Christian colonial system, W. Howitt, a man who makes a specialty of Christianity, says : "The barbarities and desperate outrages of the so-called Christian race, throughout every region of the world, and upon every people they have been able to subdue, are not to be paralleled by those of any other race, however fierce, however untaught, and however reckless of mercy and of shame, in any age of the earth." The history of the colonial administration of Holland — and Holland was the head capitalistic nation of the 17th century — "is one of the most extraordinary relations of treachery, bribery, massacre, and meanness."

The English East India Company, as is well known, obtained, besides the political rule in India, the exclusive monopoly of the tea-trade, as well as of the Chinese trade in general, and of the transport of goods to and from Europe. But the coasting trade of India and between the islands, as well as the internal trade of India, were the monopoly of the higher employés of the company. The monopolies of salt, opium, betel, and other commodities, were inexhaustible mines of wealth. The employés themselves fixed the price and plundered at will the unhappy Hindus. The Governor-General took part in this private traffic. Great fortunes sprang up like mushrooms in a day ; primitive accumulation went on without the advance of a shilling.

The treatment of the aborigines was, naturally, most frightful in plantation-colonies destined for export trade only, such as the West Indies, and in rich and well-populated countries, such as Mexico and India, that were given over to plunder. But even in the colonies properly so-called, the Christian character of primitive accumulation did not belie itself. Those sober virtuosi of Protestantism, the Puritans of New England, in 1703, by decrees of their assembly set a premium of £40 on every Indian scalp and every captured red-skin : in 1720 a premium of £100 on every scalp ; in 1744, after Massachusetts-Bay had proclaimed a certain tribe as rebels, the following prices : for a male scalp of 12 years and upwards £100 (new currency), for a male prisoner £105, for women and children prisoners £50, for scalps of women and children £50. Some decades later, the colonial system took its revenge on the descendants of the pious pilgrim fathers, who had grown seditious in the meantime. At English instigation and for English pay they were tomahawked by red-skins. The British Parliament proclaimed blood-hounds and scalping as "means that God and Nature had given into its hand."

The colonial system ripened, like a hot-house, trade and navigation. The "societies Monopolia" of Luther were powerful levers for concentration of capital. The colonies secured a market for the budding manufactures, and, through the monopoly of the market, an increased accumulation. The treasures captured outside Europe by undisguised looting, enslavement, and murder, floated back to the mother-country and were there turned into capital. Holland, which first fully developed the colonial system, in 1648 stood already in the acme of its commercial greatness. By 1648, the people of Holland were more overworked, poorer and more brutally oppressed than those of all the rest of Europe put together.

The system of public credit, *i.e.*, of national debts, whose origin we discover in Genoa and Venice as early as the Middle Ages, took possession of Europe generally during the manufacturing period. The colonial system with its maritime trade and commercial wars served as a forcing-house for it. Thus it first took root in Holland. National debts, *i.e.*, the alienation of the State — whether despotic, constitutional, or republican — marked with its stamp the capitalistic era. The only part of the so-called national wealth that actually enters into the collective possessions of modern peoples is — their national debt. The public debt becomes one of the most powerful levers of primitive accumulation. As with the stroke of an enchanter's wand, it endows barren money with the power of breeding and thus turns it into capital, without the necessity of its exposing itself to the troubles and risks inseparable from its employment in industry or even in usury.

With the national debt arose an international credit
system, which often conceals one of the sources of
primitive accumulation. Thus the villainies of the Vene-
tian thieving system formed one of the secret bases of
the capital-wealth of Holland to whom Venice in her
decadence lent large sums of money. So also was it with
Holland and England. By the beginning of the 18th
century the Dutch manufactures were far outstripped.
Holland had ceased to be the nation preponderant in
commerce and industry. One of its main lines of business, therefore, from 1701–1776, is the lending out of
enormous amounts of capital, especially to its great rival
England. The same thing is going on today between
England and the United States.

The system of protection was an artificial means of
manufacturing manufacturers, of expropriating independent labourers, of capitalising the national means of
production and subsistence, of forcibly abbreviating the
transition from the mediæval to the modern mode of
production. The European states tore one another to
pieces about the patent of this invention, and, once entered into the service of the surplus-value makers, did
not merely lay under contribution in the pursuit of this
purpose their own people, indirectly through protective
duties, directly through export premiums. The primitive industrial capital, here, came in part directly out of
the state treasury.

Colonial system, public debts, heavy taxes, protection, commercial wars, &c., these children of the true
manufacturing period, increase gigantically during the
infancy of Modern Industry. The birth of the latter is
heralded by a great slaughter of the innocents. A great
deal of capital, which appears today in the United States
without any certificate of birth, was yesterday, in England, the capitalised blood of children.

"From the different parish workhouses of London,
Birmingham, and elsewhere, many, many thousands of
these little, hapless creatures were sent down into the

north, being from the age of 7 to the age of 13 or 14 years old. The custom was for the master to clothe his apprentices and to feed and lodge them in an "apprentice house" near the factory; overseers were appointed to see to the works, whose interest it was to work the children to the utmost, because their pay was in proportion to the quantity of work that they could exact. Cruelty was, of course, the consequence. . . In many of the manufacturing districts, but particularly, I am afraid, in Lancashire, cruelties the most heart-rending were practised upon the unoffending and friendless creatures. They were harassed to the brink of death by excess of labour . . . were flogged, fettered, and tortured in the most exquisite refinement of cruelty ; . . . they were in many cases starved to the bone while flogged to their work and . . . even in some instances . . . were driven to commit suicide. . . The beautiful and romantic valleys of Derbyshire, Nottinghamshire, and Lancashire, secluded from the public eye, became the dismal solitudes of torture, and of many a murder. The profits of manufactures were enormous ; but this only whetted the appetite that it should have satisfied, and therefore the manufacturers had recourse to an expedient that seemed to secure to them those profits without any possibility of limit ; they began the practice of what is termed "night-working," that is, having tired one set of hands, by working them throughout the day, they had another set ready to go on working throughout the night ; the day-set getting into the beds that the night-set had just quitted, and in their turn again, the night-set getting into the beds that the day-set quitted in the morning. It is a common tradition in Lancashire, that the beds *never get cold*."

What does the primitive accumulation of capital, *i.e.,* its historical genesis, resolve itself into ? In so far as it is not immediate transformation of slaves and serfs into wage-labourers, and therefore a mere change of form,

it only means the expropriation of the immediate producers, *i.e.*, the dissolution of private property based on
the labour of its owner. This mode of production presupposes parcelling of the soil, and scattering of the
other means of production. As it excludes the concentration of these means of production, so also it excludes co-operation, division of labour within each separate process of production, the control over, and the
productive application of the forces of Nature by society, and the free development of the social productive
powers. At a certain stage of development it brings
forth the material agencies for its own dissolution. From
that moment new forces and new passions spring up in
the bosom of society ; but the old social organisation
fetters them and keeps them down. It must be annihilated ; it is annihilated. Its annihilation, the transformation of the individualised and scattered means of production into socially concentrated ones, of the pigmy
property of the many into the huge property of the
few, the expropriation of the great mass of the people
from the soil, from the means of subsistence, and from
the means of labour, this fearful and painful expropriation of the mass of the people forms the prelude to the
history of capital. It comprises a series of forcible methods, of which we have passed in review only those
that have been epoch-making as methods of the primitive accumulation of capital. The expropriation of the
immediate producers was accomplished with merciless
Vandalism, and under the stimulus of passions the most
infamous, the most sordid, the pettiest, the most meanly
odious. Self-earned private property, that is based, so
to say, on the fusing together of the isolated, independent labouring-individual with the conditions of his labour, is supplanted by capitalistic private property,
which rests on exploitation of the nominally free labour
of others, *i.e.*, on wages-labour.

As soon as this process of transformation has sufficiently decomposed the old society from top to bottom,

as soon as the labourers are turned into proletarians, their means of labour into capital, as soon as the capitalist mode of production stands on its own feet, then the further socialisation of labour and further transformation of the land and other means of production into socially exploited and, therefore, common means of production, as well as the further expropriation of private proprietors, takes a new form. That which is now to be expropriated is no longer the labourer working for himself, but the capitalist exploiting many labourers.

This expropriation is accomplished by the action of the immanent laws of capitalistic production itself, by the centralisation of capital. One capitalist always kills many. Hand in hand with this centralisation, or this expropriation of many capitalists by few, develope, on an ever extending scale, the co-operative form of the labour-process, the conscious technical application of science, the methodical cultivation of the soil, the transformation of the instruments of labour into instruments of labour only usable in common, the economising of all means of production by their use as the means of production of combined, socialised labour, the entanglement of all peoples in the net of the world-market, and this, the international character of the capitalistic regime. Along with the constantly diminishing number of the magnates of capital, who usurp and monopolise all advantages of this process of transformation, grows the mass of misery, oppression, slavery, degradation, exploitation ; but with this too grows the revolt of the working class, a class always increasing in numbers, and disciplined, united, organised by the very mechanism of the process of capitalist production itself. The monopoly of capital becomes a fetter upon the mode of production, which has sprung up and flourished along with, and under it. Centralisation of the means of production and socialisation of labour at last reach a point where they become incompatible with their capitalist integument. This integument is burst asunder. The knell of capitalist private property sounds. The expropriators are expropriated.

The capitalist mode of appropriation, the result of the capitalist mode of production, produces capitalist private property. This is the first negation of individual private property, as founded on the labour of the proprietor. But capitalist production begets, with the inexorability of a law of Nature, its own negation. It is the negation of negation. This does not re-establish private property for the producer, but gives him individual property based on the acquisitions of the capitalist era : *i.e.*, on co-operation and the possession in common of the land and of the means of production.

In the former case, we had the expropriation of the mass of the people by a few usurpers ; in the latter, we have the expropriation of a few usurpers by the mass of the people.

A CATALOG OF SELECTED
DOVER BOOKS
IN ALL FIELDS OF INTEREST

A CATALOG OF SELECTED DOVER
BOOKS IN ALL FIELDS OF INTEREST

CONCERNING THE SPIRITUAL IN ART, Wassily Kandinsky. Pioneering work by father of abstract art. Thoughts on color theory, nature of art. Analysis of earlier masters. 12 illustrations. 80pp. of text. 5⅜ x 8½. 0-486-23411-8

CELTIC ART: The Methods of Construction, George Bain. Simple geometric techniques for making Celtic interlacements, spirals, Kells-type initials, animals, humans, etc. Over 500 illustrations. 160pp. 9 x 12. (Available in U.S. only.) 0-486-22923-8

AN ATLAS OF ANATOMY FOR ARTISTS, Fritz Schider. Most thorough reference work on art anatomy in the world. Hundreds of illustrations, including selections from works by Vesalius, Leonardo, Goya, Ingres, Michelangelo, others. 593 illustrations. 192pp. 7⅛ x 10¼. 0-486-20241-0

CELTIC HAND STROKE-BY-STROKE (Irish Half-Uncial from "The Book of Kells"): An Arthur Baker Calligraphy Manual, Arthur Baker. Complete guide to creating each letter of the alphabet in distinctive Celtic manner. Covers hand position, strokes, pens, inks, paper, more. Illustrated. 48pp. 8¼ x 11. 0-486-24336-2

EASY ORIGAMI, John Montroll. Charming collection of 32 projects (hat, cup, pelican, piano, swan, many more) specially designed for the novice origami hobbyist. Clearly illustrated easy-to-follow instructions insure that even beginning papercrafters will achieve successful results. 48pp. 8¼ x 11. 0-486-27298-2

BLOOMINGDALE'S ILLUSTRATED 1886 CATALOG: Fashions, Dry Goods and Housewares, Bloomingdale Brothers. Famed merchants' extremely rare catalog depicting about 1,700 products: clothing, housewares, firearms, dry goods, jewelry, more. Invaluable for dating, identifying vintage items. Also, copyright-free graphics for artists, designers. Co-published with Henry Ford Museum & Greenfield Village. 160pp. 8¼ x 11. 0-486-25780-0

THE ART OF WORLDLY WISDOM, Baltasar Gracian. "Think with the few and speak with the many," "Friends are a second existence," and "Be able to forget" are among this 1637 volume's 300 pithy maxims. A perfect source of mental and spiritual refreshment, it can be opened at random and appreciated either in brief or at length. 128pp. 5⅜ x 8½. 0-486-44034-6

JOHNSON'S DICTIONARY: A Modern Selection, Samuel Johnson (E. L. McAdam and George Milne, eds.). This modern version reduces the original 1755 edition's 2,300 pages of definitions and literary examples to a more manageable length, retaining the verbal pleasure and historical curiosity of the original. 480pp. 5³⁄₁₆ x 8¼. 0-486-44089-3

ADVENTURES OF HUCKLEBERRY FINN, Mark Twain, Illustrated by E. W. Kemble. A work of eternal richness and complexity, a source of ongoing critical debate, and a literary landmark, Twain's 1885 masterpiece about a barefoot boy's journey of self-discovery has enthralled readers around the world. This handsome clothbound reproduction of the first edition features all 174 of the original black-and-white illustrations. 368pp. 5⅜ x 8½. 0-486-44322-1

CATALOG OF DOVER BOOKS

STICKLEY CRAFTSMAN FURNITURE CATALOGS, Gustav Stickley and L. &
J. G. Stickley. Beautiful, functional furniture in two authentic catalogs from 1910. 594
illustrations, including 277 photos, show settles, rockers, armchairs, reclining chairs,
bookcases, desks, tables. 183pp. 6½ x 9¼.   0-486-23838-5

AMERICAN LOCOMOTIVES IN HISTORIC PHOTOGRAPHS: 1858 to 1949,
Ron Ziel (ed.). A rare collection of 126 meticulously detailed official photographs,
called "builder portraits," of American locomotives that majestically chronicle the
rise of steam locomotive power in America. Introduction. Detailed captions. xi+
129pp. 9 x 12.   0-486-27393-8

AMERICA'S LIGHTHOUSES: An Illustrated History, Francis Ross Holland, Jr.
Delightfully written, profusely illustrated fact-filled survey of over 200 American lighthouses since 1716. History, anecdotes, technological advances, more. 240pp. 8 x 10¾.
                                                                           0-486-25576-X

TOWARDS A NEW ARCHITECTURE, Le Corbusier. Pioneering manifesto by
founder of "International School." Technical and aesthetic theories, views of industry, economics, relation of form to function, "mass-production split" and much more. Profusely
illustrated. 320pp. 6⅛ x 9¼. (Available in U.S. only.)   0-486-25023-7

HOW THE OTHER HALF LIVES, Jacob Riis. Famous journalistic record, exposing poverty and degradation of New York slums around 1900, by major social
reformer. 100 striking and influential photographs. 233pp. 10 x 7⅞.   0-486-22012-5

FRUIT KEY AND TWIG KEY TO TREES AND SHRUBS, William M. Harlow.
One of the handiest and most widely used identification aids. Fruit key covers 120
deciduous and evergreen species; twig key 160 deciduous species. Easily used. Over
300 photographs. 126pp. 5⅜ x 8½.   0-486-20511-8

COMMON BIRD SONGS, Dr. Donald J. Borror. Songs of 60 most common U.S.
birds: robins, sparrows, cardinals, bluejays, finches, more—arranged in order of
increasing complexity. Up to 9 variations of songs of each species.
                                        Cassette and manual 0-486-99911-4

ORCHIDS AS HOUSE PLANTS, Rebecca Tyson Northen. Grow cattleyas and
many other kinds of orchids—in a window, in a case, or under artificial light. 63 illustrations. 148pp. 5⅜ x 8½.   0-486-23261-1

MONSTER MAZES, Dave Phillips. Masterful mazes at four levels of difficulty.
Avoid deadly perils and evil creatures to find magical treasures. Solutions for all 32
exciting illustrated puzzles. 48pp. 8¼ x 11.   0-486-26005-4

MOZART'S DON GIOVANNI (DOVER OPERA LIBRETTO SERIES),
Wolfgang Amadeus Mozart. Introduced and translated by Ellen H. Bleiler. Standard
Italian libretto, with complete English translation. Convenient and thoroughly
portable—an ideal companion for reading along with a recording or the performance
itself. Introduction. List of characters. Plot summary. 121pp. 5¼ x 8½. 0-486-24944-1

FRANK LLOYD WRIGHT'S DANA HOUSE, Donald Hoffmann. Pictorial essay
of residential masterpiece with over 160 interior and exterior photos, plans, elevations, sketches and studies. 128pp. 9¹/₄ x 10¾.   0-486-29120-0

THE CLARINET AND CLARINET PLAYING, David Pino. Lively, comprehensive work features suggestions about technique, musicianship, and musical interpretation, as well as guidelines for teaching, making your own reeds, and preparing for public performance. Includes an intriguing look at clarinet history. "A godsend," *The Clarinet,* Journal of the International Clarinet Society. Appendixes. 7 illus. 320pp. 5⅜ x 8½. 0-486-40270-3

HOLLYWOOD GLAMOR PORTRAITS, John Kobal (ed.). 145 photos from 1926-49. Harlow, Gable, Bogart, Bacall; 94 stars in all. Full background on photographers, technical aspects. 160pp. 8⅜ x 11¼. 0-486-23352-9

THE RAVEN AND OTHER FAVORITE POEMS, Edgar Allan Poe. Over 40 of the author's most memorable poems: "The Bells," "Ulalume," "Israfel," "To Helen," "The Conqueror Worm," "Eldorado," "Annabel Lee," many more. Alphabetic lists of titles and first lines. 64pp. 5$\frac{3}{16}$ x 8¼. 0-486-26685-0

PERSONAL MEMOIRS OF U. S. GRANT, Ulysses Simpson Grant. Intelligent, deeply moving firsthand account of Civil War campaigns, considered by many the finest military memoirs ever written. Includes letters, historic photographs, maps and more. 528pp. 6⅛ x 9¼. 0-486-28587-1

ANCIENT EGYPTIAN MATERIALS AND INDUSTRIES, A. Lucas and J. Harris. Fascinating, comprehensive, thoroughly documented text describes this ancient civilization's vast resources and the processes that incorporated them in daily life, including the use of animal products, building materials, cosmetics, perfumes and incense, fibers, glazed ware, glass and its manufacture, materials used in the mummification process, and much more. 544pp. 6⅛ x 9¼. (Available in U.S. only.) 0-486-40446-3

RUSSIAN STORIES/RUSSKIE RASSKAZY: A Dual-Language Book, edited by Gleb Struve. Twelve tales by such masters as Chekhov, Tolstoy, Dostoevsky, Pushkin, others. Excellent word-for-word English translations on facing pages, plus teaching and study aids, Russian/English vocabulary, biographical/critical introductions, more. 416pp. 5⅜ x 8½. 0-486-26244-8

PHILADELPHIA THEN AND NOW: 60 Sites Photographed in the Past and Present, Kenneth Finkel and Susan Oyama. Rare photographs of City Hall, Logan Square, Independence Hall, Betsy Ross House, other landmarks juxtaposed with contemporary views. Captures changing face of historic city. Introduction. Captions. 128pp. 8¼ x 11. 0-486-25790-8

NORTH AMERICAN INDIAN LIFE: Customs and Traditions of 23 Tribes, Elsie Clews Parsons (ed.). 27 fictionalized essays by noted anthropologists examine religion, customs, government, additional facets of life among the Winnebago, Crow, Zuni, Eskimo, other tribes. 480pp. 6⅛ x 9¼. 0-486-27377-6

TECHNICAL MANUAL AND DICTIONARY OF CLASSICAL BALLET, Gail Grant. Defines, explains, comments on steps, movements, poses and concepts. 15-page pictorial section. Basic book for student, viewer. 127pp. 5⅜ x 8½. 0-486-21843-0

THE MALE AND FEMALE FIGURE IN MOTION: 60 Classic Photographic Sequences, Eadweard Muybridge. 60 true-action photographs of men and women walking, running, climbing, bending, turning, etc., reproduced from rare 19th-century masterpiece. vi + 121pp. 9 x 12. 0-486-24745-7

ANIMALS: 1,419 Copyright-Free Illustrations of Mammals, Birds, Fish, Insects, etc., Jim Harter (ed.). Clear wood engravings present, in extremely lifelike poses, over 1,000 species of animals. One of the most extensive pictorial sourcebooks of its kind. Captions. Index. 284pp. 9 x 12. 0-486-23766-4

1001 QUESTIONS ANSWERED ABOUT THE SEASHORE, N. J. Berrill and Jacquelyn Berrill. Queries answered about dolphins, sea snails, sponges, starfish, fishes, shore birds, many others. Covers appearance, breeding, growth, feeding, much more. 305pp. 5¼ x 8¼. 0-486-23366-9

ATTRACTING BIRDS TO YOUR YARD, William J. Weber. Easy-to-follow guide offers advice on how to attract the greatest diversity of birds: birdhouses, feeders, water and waterers, much more. 96pp. 5³⁄₁₆ x 8¼. 0-486-28927-3

MEDICINAL AND OTHER USES OF NORTH AMERICAN PLANTS: A Historical Survey with Special Reference to the Eastern Indian Tribes, Charlotte Erichsen-Brown. Chronological historical citations document 500 years of usage of plants, trees, shrubs native to eastern Canada, northeastern U.S. Also complete identifying information. 343 illustrations. 544pp. 6½ x 9¼. 0-486-25951-X

STORYBOOK MAZES, Dave Phillips. 23 stories and mazes on two-page spreads: Wizard of Oz, Treasure Island, Robin Hood, etc. Solutions. 64pp. 8¼ x 11.
0-486-23628-5

AMERICAN NEGRO SONGS: 230 Folk Songs and Spirituals, Religious and Secular, John W. Work. This authoritative study traces the African influences of songs sung and played by black Americans at work, in church, and as entertainment. The author discusses the lyric significance of such songs as "Swing Low, Sweet Chariot," "John Henry," and others and offers the words and music for 230 songs. Bibliography. Index of Song Titles. 272pp. 6½ x 9¼. 0-486-40271-1

MOVIE-STAR PORTRAITS OF THE FORTIES, John Kobal (ed.). 163 glamor, studio photos of 106 stars of the 1940s: Rita Hayworth, Ava Gardner, Marlon Brando, Clark Gable, many more. 176pp. 8⅜ x 11¼. 0-486-23546-7

YEKL and THE IMPORTED BRIDEGROOM AND OTHER STORIES OF YIDDISH NEW YORK, Abraham Cahan. Film Hester Street based on *Yekl* (1896). Novel, other stories among first about Jewish immigrants on N.Y.'s East Side. 240pp. 5⅜ x 8½. 0-486-22427-9

SELECTED POEMS, Walt Whitman. Generous sampling from *Leaves of Grass*. Twenty-four poems include "I Hear America Singing," "Song of the Open Road," "I Sing the Body Electric," "When Lilacs Last in the Dooryard Bloom'd," "O Captain! My Captain!"–all reprinted from an authoritative edition. Lists of titles and first lines. 128pp. 5³⁄₁₆ x 8¼. 0-486-26878-0

SONGS OF EXPERIENCE: Facsimile Reproduction with 26 Plates in Full Color, William Blake. 26 full-color plates from a rare 1826 edition. Includes "The Tyger," "London," "Holy Thursday," and other poems. Printed text of poems. 48pp. 5¼ x 7.
0-486-24636-1

THE BEST TALES OF HOFFMANN, E. T. A. Hoffmann. 10 of Hoffmann's most important stories: "Nutcracker and the King of Mice," "The Golden Flowerpot," etc. 458pp. 5⅜ x 8½. 0-486-21793-0

THE BOOK OF TEA, Kakuzo Okakura. Minor classic of the Orient: entertaining, charming explanation, interpretation of traditional Japanese culture in terms of tea ceremony. 94pp. 5⅜ x 8½. 0-486-20070-1

FRENCH STORIES/CONTES FRANÇAIS: A Dual-Language Book, Wallace Fowlie. Ten stories by French masters, Voltaire to Camus: "Micromegas" by Voltaire; "The Atheist's Mass" by Balzac; "Minuet" by de Maupassant; "The Guest" by Camus, six more. Excellent English translations on facing pages. Also French-English vocabulary list, exercises, more. 352pp. 5⅜ x 8½. 0-486-26443-2

CHICAGO AT THE TURN OF THE CENTURY IN PHOTOGRAPHS: 122 Historic Views from the Collections of the Chicago Historical Society, Larry A. Viskochil. Rare large-format prints offer detailed views of City Hall, State Street, the Loop, Hull House, Union Station, many other landmarks, circa 1904-1913. Introduction. Captions. Maps. 144pp. 9⅜ x 12¼. 0-486-24656-6

OLD BROOKLYN IN EARLY PHOTOGRAPHS, 1865-1929, William Lee Younger. Luna Park, Gravesend race track, construction of Grand Army Plaza, moving of Hotel Brighton, etc. 157 previously unpublished photographs. 165pp. 8⅞ x 11¾. 0-486-23587-4

THE MYTHS OF THE NORTH AMERICAN INDIANS, Lewis Spence. Rich anthology of the myths and legends of the Algonquins, Iroquois, Pawnees and Sioux, prefaced by an extensive historical and ethnological commentary. 36 illustrations. 480pp. 5⅜ x 8½. 0-486-25967-6

AN ENCYCLOPEDIA OF BATTLES: Accounts of Over 1,560 Battles from 1479 B.C. to the Present, David Eggenberger. Essential details of every major battle in recorded history from the first battle of Megiddo in 1479 B.C. to Grenada in 1984. List of Battle Maps. New Appendix covering the years 1967-1984. Index. 99 illustrations. 544pp. 6½ x 9¼. 0-486-24913-1

SAILING ALONE AROUND THE WORLD, Captain Joshua Slocum. First man to sail around the world, alone, in small boat. One of great feats of seamanship told in delightful manner. 67 illustrations. 294pp. 5⅜ x 8½. 0-486-20326-3

ANARCHISM AND OTHER ESSAYS, Emma Goldman. Powerful, penetrating, prophetic essays on direct action, role of minorities, prison reform, puritan hypocrisy, violence, etc. 271pp. 5⅜ x 8½. 0-486-22484-8

MYTHS OF THE HINDUS AND BUDDHISTS, Ananda K. Coomaraswamy and Sister Nivedita. Great stories of the epics; deeds of Krishna, Shiva, taken from puranas, Vedas, folk tales; etc. 32 illustrations. 400pp. 5⅜ x 8½. 0-486-21759-0

MY BONDAGE AND MY FREEDOM, Frederick Douglass. Born a slave, Douglass became outspoken force in antislavery movement. The best of Douglass' autobiographies. Graphic description of slave life. 464pp. 5⅜ x 8½. 0-486-22457-0

FOLLOWING THE EQUATOR: A Journey Around the World, Mark Twain. Fascinating humorous account of 1897 voyage to Hawaii, Australia, India, New Zealand, etc. Ironic, bemused reports on peoples, customs, climate, flora and fauna, politics, much more. 197 illustrations. 720pp. 5⅜ x 8½. 0-486-26113-1

THE PEOPLE CALLED SHAKERS, Edward D. Andrews. Definitive study of Shakers: origins, beliefs, practices, dances, social organization, furniture and crafts, etc. 33 illustrations. 351pp. 5⅜ x 8½. 0-486-21081-2

THE MYTHS OF GREECE AND ROME, H. A. Guerber. A classic of mythology, generously illustrated, long prized for its simple, graphic, accurate retelling of the principal myths of Greece and Rome, and for its commentary on their origins and significance. With 64 illustrations by Michelangelo, Raphael, Titian, Rubens, Canova, Bernini and others. 480pp. 5⅜ x 8½. 0-486-27584-1

PSYCHOLOGY OF MUSIC, Carl E. Seashore. Classic work discusses music as a medium from psychological viewpoint. Clear treatment of physical acoustics, auditory apparatus, sound perception, development of musical skills, nature of musical feeling, host of other topics. 88 figures. 408pp. 5⅜ x 8½. 0-486-21851-1

LIFE IN ANCIENT EGYPT, Adolf Erman. Fullest, most thorough, detailed older account with much not in more recent books, domestic life, religion, magic, medicine, commerce, much more. Many illustrations reproduce tomb paintings, carvings, hieroglyphs, etc. 597pp. 5⅜ x 8½. 0-486-22632-8

SUNDIALS, Their Theory and Construction, Albert Waugh. Far and away the best, most thorough coverage of ideas, mathematics concerned, types, construction, adjusting anywhere. Simple, nontechnical treatment allows even children to build several of these dials. Over 100 illustrations. 230pp. 5⅜ x 8½. 0-486-22947-5

THEORETICAL HYDRODYNAMICS, L. M. Milne-Thomson. Classic exposition of the mathematical theory of fluid motion, applicable to both hydrodynamics and aerodynamics. Over 600 exercises. 768pp. 6⅛ x 9¼. 0-486-68970-0

OLD-TIME VIGNETTES IN FULL COLOR, Carol Belanger Grafton (ed.). Over 390 charming, often sentimental illustrations, selected from archives of Victorian graphics—pretty women posing, children playing, food, flowers, kittens and puppies, smiling cherubs, birds and butterflies, much more. All copyright-free. 48pp. 9¼ x 12¼. 0-486-27269-9

PERSPECTIVE FOR ARTISTS, Rex Vicat Cole. Depth, perspective of sky and sea, shadows, much more, not usually covered. 391 diagrams, 81 reproductions of drawings and paintings. 279pp. 5⅜ x 8½. 0-486-22487-2

DRAWING THE LIVING FIGURE, Joseph Sheppard. Innovative approach to artistic anatomy focuses on specifics of surface anatomy, rather than muscles and bones. Over 170 drawings of live models in front, back and side views, and in widely varying poses. Accompanying diagrams. 177 illustrations. Introduction. Index. 144pp. 8⅜ x 11¼. 0-486-26723-7

GOTHIC AND OLD ENGLISH ALPHABETS: 100 Complete Fonts, Dan X. Solo. Add power, elegance to posters, signs, other graphics with 100 stunning copyright-free alphabets: Blackstone, Dolbey, Germania, 97 more—including many lower-case, numerals, punctuation marks. 104pp. 8⅛ x 11. 0-486-24695-7

THE BOOK OF WOOD CARVING, Charles Marshall Sayers. Finest book for beginners discusses fundamentals and offers 34 designs. "Absolutely first rate . . . well thought out and well executed."–E. J. Tangerman. 118pp. 7¾ x 10⅝. 0-486-23654-4

ILLUSTRATED CATALOG OF CIVIL WAR MILITARY GOODS: Union Army Weapons, Insignia, Uniform Accessories, and Other Equipment, Schuyler, Hartley, and Graham. Rare, profusely illustrated 1846 catalog includes Union Army uniform and dress regulations, arms and ammunition, coats, insignia, flags, swords, rifles, etc. 226 illustrations. 160pp. 9 x 12. 0-486-24939-5

WOMEN'S FASHIONS OF THE EARLY 1900s: An Unabridged Republication of "New York Fashions, 1909," National Cloak & Suit Co. Rare catalog of mail-order fashions documents women's and children's clothing styles shortly after the turn of the century. Captions offer full descriptions, prices. Invaluable resource for fashion, costume historians. Approximately 725 illustrations. 128pp. 8⅜ x 11¼. 0-486-27276-1

CATALOG OF DOVER BOOKS

HOW TO DO BEADWORK, Mary White. Fundamental book on craft from simple projects to five-bead chains and woven works. 106 illustrations. 142pp. 5⅜ x 8.
0-486-20697-1

THE 1912 AND 1915 GUSTAV STICKLEY FURNITURE CATALOGS, Gustav Stickley. With over 200 detailed illustrations and descriptions, these two catalogs are essential reading and reference materials and identification guides for Stickley furniture. Captions cite materials, dimensions and prices. 112pp. 6½ x 9¼. 0-486-26676-1

EARLY AMERICAN LOCOMOTIVES, John H. White, Jr. Finest locomotive engravings from early 19th century: historical (1804–74), main-line (after 1870), special, foreign, etc. 147 plates. 142pp. 11⅜ x 8¼. 0-486-22772-3

LITTLE BOOK OF EARLY AMERICAN CRAFTS AND TRADES, Peter Stockham (ed.). 1807 children's book explains crafts and trades: baker, hatter, cooper, potter, and many others. 23 copperplate illustrations. 140pp. 4⅝ x 6.
0-486-23336-7

VICTORIAN FASHIONS AND COSTUMES FROM HARPER'S BAZAR, 1867–1898, Stella Blum (ed.). Day costumes, evening wear, sports clothes, shoes, hats, other accessories in over 1,000 detailed engravings. 320pp. 9⅜ x 12¼.
0-486-22990-4

THE LONG ISLAND RAIL ROAD IN EARLY PHOTOGRAPHS, Ron Ziel. Over 220 rare photos, informative text document origin (1844) and development of rail service on Long Island. Vintage views of early trains, locomotives, stations, passengers, crews, much more. Captions. 8⅞ x 11¾. 0-486-26301-0

VOYAGE OF THE LIBERDADE, Joshua Slocum. Great 19th-century mariner's thrilling, first-hand account of the wreck of his ship off South America, the 35-foot boat he built from the wreckage, and its remarkable voyage home. 128pp. 5⅜ x 8½.
0-486-40022-0

TEN BOOKS ON ARCHITECTURE, Vitruvius. The most important book ever written on architecture. Early Roman aesthetics, technology, classical orders, site selection, all other aspects. Morgan translation. 331pp. 5⅜ x 8½. 0-486-20645-9

THE HUMAN FIGURE IN MOTION, Eadweard Muybridge. More than 4,500 stopped-action photos, in action series, showing undraped men, women, children jumping, lying down, throwing, sitting, wrestling, carrying, etc. 390pp. 7⅞ x 10⅝.
0-486-20204-6 Clothbd.

TREES OF THE EASTERN AND CENTRAL UNITED STATES AND CANADA, William M. Harlow. Best one-volume guide to 140 trees. Full descriptions, woodlore, range, etc. Over 600 illustrations. Handy size. 288pp. 4½ x 6⅜. 0-486-20395-6

GROWING AND USING HERBS AND SPICES, Milo Miloradovich. Versatile handbook provides all the information needed for cultivation and use of all the herbs and spices available in North America. 4 illustrations. Index. Glossary. 236pp. 5⅜ x 8½.
0-486-25058-X

BIG BOOK OF MAZES AND LABYRINTHS, Walter Shepherd. 50 mazes and labyrinths in all–classical, solid, ripple, and more–in one great volume. Perfect inexpensive puzzler for clever youngsters. Full solutions. 112pp. 8¼ x 11. 0-486-22951-3

PIANO TUNING, J. Cree Fischer. Clearest, best book for beginner, amateur. Simple repairs, raising dropped notes, tuning by easy method of flattened fifths. No previous skills needed. 4 illustrations. 201pp. 5⅜ x 8½. 0-486-23267-0

HINTS TO SINGERS, Lillian Nordica. Selecting the right teacher, developing confidence, overcoming stage fright, and many other important skills receive thoughtful discussion in this indispensible guide, written by a world-famous diva of four decades' experience. 96pp. $5\frac{3}{8}$ x $8\frac{1}{2}$. 0-486-40094-8

THE COMPLETE NONSENSE OF EDWARD LEAR, Edward Lear. All nonsense limericks, zany alphabets, Owl and Pussycat, songs, nonsense botany, etc., illustrated by Lear. Total of 320pp. $5\frac{3}{8}$ x $8\frac{1}{2}$. (Available in U.S. only.) 0-486-20167-8

VICTORIAN PARLOUR POETRY: An Annotated Anthology, Michael R. Turner. 117 gems by Longfellow, Tennyson, Browning, many lesser-known poets. "The Village Blacksmith," "Curfew Must Not Ring Tonight," "Only a Baby Small," dozens more, often difficult to find elsewhere. Index of poets, titles, first lines. xxiii + 325pp. $5\frac{3}{8}$ x $8\frac{1}{4}$. 0-486-27044-0

DUBLINERS, James Joyce. Fifteen stories offer vivid, tightly focused observations of the lives of Dublin's poorer classes. At least one, "The Dead," is considered a masterpiece. Reprinted complete and unabridged from standard edition. 160pp. $5\frac{3}{16}$ x $8\frac{1}{4}$. 0-486-26870-5

GREAT WEIRD TALES: 14 Stories by Lovecraft, Blackwood, Machen and Others, S. T. Joshi (ed.). 14 spellbinding tales, including "The Sin Eater," by Fiona McLeod, "The Eye Above the Mantel," by Frank Belknap Long, as well as renowned works by R. H. Barlow, Lord Dunsany, Arthur Machen, W. C. Morrow and eight other masters of the genre. 256pp. $5\frac{3}{8}$ x $8\frac{1}{2}$. (Available in U.S. only.) 0-486-40436-6

THE BOOK OF THE SACRED MAGIC OF ABRAMELIN THE MAGE, translated by S. MacGregor Mathers. Medieval manuscript of ceremonial magic. Basic document in Aleister Crowley, Golden Dawn groups. 268pp. $5\frac{3}{8}$ x $8\frac{1}{2}$. 0-486-23211-5

THE BATTLES THAT CHANGED HISTORY, Fletcher Pratt. Eminent historian profiles 16 crucial conflicts, ancient to modern, that changed the course of civilization. 352pp. $5\frac{3}{8}$ x $8\frac{1}{2}$. 0-486-41129-X

NEW RUSSIAN-ENGLISH AND ENGLISH-RUSSIAN DICTIONARY, M. A. O'Brien. This is a remarkably handy Russian dictionary, containing a surprising amount of information, including over 70,000 entries. 366pp. $4\frac{1}{2}$ x $6\frac{1}{8}$. 0-486-20208-9

NEW YORK IN THE FORTIES, Andreas Feininger. 162 brilliant photographs by the well-known photographer, formerly with *Life* magazine. Commuters, shoppers, Times Square at night, much else from city at its peak. Captions by John von Hartz. 181pp. $9\frac{1}{4}$ x $10\frac{3}{4}$. 0-486-23585-8

INDIAN SIGN LANGUAGE, William Tomkins. Over 525 signs developed by Sioux and other tribes. Written instructions and diagrams. Also 290 pictographs. 111pp. $6\frac{1}{8}$ x $9\frac{1}{4}$. 0-486-22029-X

ANATOMY: A Complete Guide for Artists, Joseph Sheppard. A master of figure drawing shows artists how to render human anatomy convincingly. Over 460 illustrations. 224pp. $8\frac{3}{8}$ x $11\frac{1}{4}$. 0-486-27279-6

MEDIEVAL CALLIGRAPHY: Its History and Technique, Marc Drogin. Spirited history, comprehensive instruction manual covers 13 styles (ca. 4th century through 15th). Excellent photographs; directions for duplicating medieval techniques with modern tools. 224pp. $8\frac{3}{8}$ x $11\frac{1}{4}$. 0-486-26142-5

CATALOG OF DOVER BOOKS

DRIED FLOWERS: How to Prepare Them, Sarah Whitlock and Martha Rankin. Complete instructions on how to use silica gel, meal and borax, perlite aggregate, sand and borax, glycerine and water to create attractive permanent flower arrangements. 12 illustrations. 32pp. 5⅜ x 8½. 0-486-21802-3

EASY-TO-MAKE BIRD FEEDERS FOR WOODWORKERS, Scott D. Campbell. Detailed, simple-to-use guide for designing, constructing, caring for and using feeders. Text, illustrations for 12 classic and contemporary designs. 96pp. 5⅜ x 8½. 0-486-25847-5

THE COMPLETE BOOK OF BIRDHOUSE CONSTRUCTION FOR WOODWORKERS, Scott D. Campbell. Detailed instructions, illustrations, tables. Also data on bird habitat and instinct patterns. Bibliography. 3 tables. 63 illustrations in 15 figures. 48pp. 5¼ x 8½. 0-486-24407-5

SCOTTISH WONDER TALES FROM MYTH AND LEGEND, Donald A. Mackenzie. 16 lively tales tell of giants rumbling down mountainsides, of a magic wand that turns stone pillars into warriors, of gods and goddesses, evil hags, powerful forces and more. 240pp. 5⅜ x 8½. 0-486-29677-6

THE HISTORY OF UNDERCLOTHES, C. Willett Cunnington and Phyllis Cunnington. Fascinating, well-documented survey covering six centuries of English undergarments, enhanced with over 100 illustrations: 12th-century laced-up bodice, footed long drawers (1795), 19th-century bustles, 19th-century corsets for men, Victorian "bust improvers," much more. 272pp. 5⅜ x 8¼. 0-486-27124-2

ARTS AND CRAFTS FURNITURE: The Complete Brooks Catalog of 1912, Brooks Manufacturing Co. Photos and detailed descriptions of more than 150 now very collectible furniture designs from the Arts and Crafts movement depict davenports, settees, buffets, desks, tables, chairs, bedsteads, dressers and more, all built of solid, quarter-sawed oak. Invaluable for students and enthusiasts of antiques, Americana and the decorative arts. 80pp. 6½ x 9¼. 0-486-27471-3

WILBUR AND ORVILLE: A Biography of the Wright Brothers, Fred Howard. Definitive, crisply written study tells the full story of the brothers' lives and work. A vividly written biography, unparalleled in scope and color, that also captures the spirit of an extraordinary era. 560pp. 6⅛ x 9¼. 0-486-40297-5

THE ARTS OF THE SAILOR: Knotting, Splicing and Ropework, Hervey Garrett Smith. Indispensable shipboard reference covers tools, basic knots and useful hitches; handsewing and canvas work, more. Over 100 illustrations. Delightful reading for sea lovers. 256pp. 5⅜ x 8½. 0-486-26440-8

FRANK LLOYD WRIGHT'S FALLINGWATER: The House and Its History, Second, Revised Edition, Donald Hoffmann. A total revision—both in text and illustrations—of the standard document on Fallingwater, the boldest, most personal architectural statement of Wright's mature years, updated with valuable new material from the recently opened Frank Lloyd Wright Archives. "Fascinating"–The New York Times. 116 illustrations. 128pp. 9¼ x 10¾. 0-486-27430-6

PHOTOGRAPHIC SKETCHBOOK OF THE CIVIL WAR, Alexander Gardner. 100 photos taken on field during the Civil War. Famous shots of Manassas Harper's Ferry, Lincoln, Richmond, slave pens, etc. 244pp. 10⅝ x 8¼. 0-486-22731-6

FIVE ACRES AND INDEPENDENCE, Maurice G. Kains. Great back-to-the-land classic explains basics of self-sufficient farming. The one book to get. 95 illustrations. 397pp. 5⅜ x 8½. 0-486-20974-1

A MODERN HERBAL, Margaret Grieve. Much the fullest, most exact, most useful compilation of herbal material. Gigantic alphabetical encyclopedia, from aconite to zedoary, gives botanical information, medical properties, folklore, economic uses, much else. Indispensable to serious reader. 161 illustrations. 888pp. 6½ x 9¼. 2-vol. set. (Available in U.S. only.)   Vol. I: 0-486-22798-7   Vol. II: 0-486-22799-5

HIDDEN TREASURE MAZE BOOK, Dave Phillips. Solve 34 challenging mazes accompanied by heroic tales of adventure. Evil dragons, people-eating plants, blood-thirsty giants, many more dangerous adversaries lurk at every twist and turn. 34 mazes, stories, solutions. 48pp. 8¼ x 11.   0-486-24566-7

LETTERS OF W. A. MOZART, Wolfgang A. Mozart. Remarkable letters show bawdy wit, humor, imagination, musical insights, contemporary musical world; includes some letters from Leopold Mozart. 276pp. 5⅜ x 8½.   0-486-22859-2

BASIC PRINCIPLES OF CLASSICAL BALLET, Agrippina Vaganova. Great Russian theoretician, teacher explains methods for teaching classical ballet. 118 illustrations. 175pp. 5⅜ x 8½.   0-486-22036-2

THE JUMPING FROG, Mark Twain. Revenge edition. The original story of The Celebrated Jumping Frog of Calaveras County, a hapless French translation, and Twain's hilarious "retranslation" from the French. 12 illustrations. 66pp. 5⅜ x 8½.
                                                                              0-486-22686-7

BEST REMEMBERED POEMS, Martin Gardner (ed.). The 126 poems in this superb collection of 19th- and 20th-century British and American verse range from Shelley's "To a Skylark" to the impassioned "Renascence" of Edna St. Vincent Millay and to Edward Lear's whimsical "The Owl and the Pussycat." 224pp. 5⅜ x 8½.
                                                                              0-486-27165-X

COMPLETE SONNETS, William Shakespeare. Over 150 exquisite poems deal with love, friendship, the tyranny of time, beauty's evanescence, death and other themes in language of remarkable power, precision and beauty. Glossary of archaic terms. 80pp. 5³⁄₁₆ x 8¼.   0-486-26686-9

HISTORIC HOMES OF THE AMERICAN PRESIDENTS, Second, Revised Edition, Irvin Haas. A traveler's guide to American Presidential homes, most open to the public, depicting and describing homes occupied by every American President from George Washington to George Bush. With visiting hours, admission charges, travel routes. 175 photographs. Index. 160pp. 8¼ x 11.   0-486-26751-2

THE WIT AND HUMOR OF OSCAR WILDE, Alvin Redman (ed.). More than 1,000 ripostes, paradoxes, wisecracks: Work is the curse of the drinking classes; I can resist everything except temptation; etc. 258pp. 5⅜ x 8½.   0-486-20602-5

SHAKESPEARE LEXICON AND QUOTATION DICTIONARY, Alexander Schmidt. Full definitions, locations, shades of meaning in every word in plays and poems. More than 50,000 exact quotations. 1,485pp. 6½ x 9¼. 2-vol. set.
                        Vol. 1: 0-486-22726-X   Vol. 2: 0-486-22727-8

SELECTED POEMS, Emily Dickinson. Over 100 best-known, best-loved poems by one of America's foremost poets, reprinted from authoritative early editions. No comparable edition at this price. Index of first lines. 64pp. 5³⁄₁₆ x 8¼. 0-486-26466-1

THE INSIDIOUS DR. FU-MANCHU, Sax Rohmer. The first of the popular mystery series introduces a pair of English detectives to their archnemesis, the diabolical Dr. Fu-Manchu. Flavorful atmosphere, fast-paced action, and colorful characters enliven this classic of the genre. 208pp. 5³⁄₁₆ x 8¼.   0-486-29898-1

THE MALLEUS MALEFICARUM OF KRAMER AND SPRENGER, translated by Montague Summers. Full text of most important witchhunter's "bible," used by both Catholics and Protestants. 278pp. 6⅝ x 10. 0-486-22802-9

SPANISH STORIES/CUENTOS ESPAÑOLES: A Dual-Language Book, Angel Flores (ed.). Unique format offers 13 great stories in Spanish by Cervantes, Borges, others. Faithful English translations on facing pages. 352pp. 5⅜ x 8½.
0-486-25399-6

GARDEN CITY, LONG ISLAND, IN EARLY PHOTOGRAPHS, 1869–1919, Mildred H. Smith. Handsome treasury of 118 vintage pictures, accompanied by carefully researched captions, document the Garden City Hotel fire (1899), the Vanderbilt Cup Race (1908), the first airmail flight departing from the Nassau Boulevard Aerodrome (1911), and much more. 96pp. 8⅞ x 11¾. 0-486-40669-5

OLD QUEENS, N.Y., IN EARLY PHOTOGRAPHS, Vincent F. Seyfried and William Asadorian. Over 160 rare photographs of Maspeth, Jamaica, Jackson Heights, and other areas. Vintage views of DeWitt Clinton mansion, 1939 World's Fair and more. Captions. 192pp. 8⅞ x 11. 0-486-26358-4

CAPTURED BY THE INDIANS: 15 Firsthand Accounts, 1750-1870, Frederick Drimmer. Astounding true historical accounts of grisly torture, bloody conflicts, relentless pursuits, miraculous escapes and more, by people who lived to tell the tale. 384pp. 5⅜ x 8½. 0-486-24901-8

THE WORLD'S GREAT SPEECHES (Fourth Enlarged Edition), Lewis Copeland, Lawrence W. Lamm, and Stephen J. McKenna. Nearly 300 speeches provide public speakers with a wealth of updated quotes and inspiration–from Pericles' funeral oration and William Jennings Bryan's "Cross of Gold Speech" to Malcolm X's powerful words on the Black Revolution and Earl of Spenser's tribute to his sister, Diana, Princess of Wales. 944pp. 5⅜ x 8⅜. 0-486-40903-1

THE BOOK OF THE SWORD, Sir Richard F. Burton. Great Victorian scholar/adventurer's eloquent, erudite history of the "queen of weapons"–from prehistory to early Roman Empire. Evolution and development of early swords, variations (sabre, broadsword, cutlass, scimitar, etc.), much more. 336pp. 6⅛ x 9¼.
0-486-25434-8

AUTOBIOGRAPHY: The Story of My Experiments with Truth, Mohandas K. Gandhi. Boyhood, legal studies, purification, the growth of the Satyagraha (nonviolent protest) movement. Critical, inspiring work of the man responsible for the freedom of India. 480pp. 5⅜ x 8½. (Available in U.S. only.) 0-486-24593-4

CELTIC MYTHS AND LEGENDS, T. W. Rolleston. Masterful retelling of Irish and Welsh stories and tales. Cuchulain, King Arthur, Deirdre, the Grail, many more. First paperback edition. 58 full-page illustrations. 512pp. 5⅜ x 8½. 0-486-26507-2

THE PRINCIPLES OF PSYCHOLOGY, William James. Famous long course complete, unabridged. Stream of thought, time perception, memory, experimental methods; great work decades ahead of its time. 94 figures. 1,391pp. 5⅜ x 8½. 2-vol. set.
Vol. I: 0-486-20381-6   Vol. II: 0-486-20382-4

THE WORLD AS WILL AND REPRESENTATION, Arthur Schopenhauer. Definitive English translation of Schopenhauer's life work, correcting more than 1,000 errors, omissions in earlier translations. Translated by E. F. J. Payne. Total of 1,269pp. 5⅜ x 8½. 2-vol. set.   Vol. 1: 0-486-21761-2   Vol. 2: 0-486-21762-0

MAGIC AND MYSTERY IN TIBET, Madame Alexandra David-Neel. Experiences among lamas, magicians, sages, sorcerers, Bonpa wizards. A true psychic discovery. 32 illustrations. 321pp. 5⅜ x 8½. (Available in U.S. only.) 0-486-22682-4

THE EGYPTIAN BOOK OF THE DEAD, E. A. Wallis Budge. Complete reproduction of Ani's papyrus, finest ever found. Full hieroglyphic text, interlinear transliteration, word-for-word translation, smooth translation. 533pp. 6½ x 9¼. 0-486-21866-X

HISTORIC COSTUME IN PICTURES, Braun & Schneider. Over 1,450 costumed figures in clearly detailed engravings–from dawn of civilization to end of 19th century. Captions. Many folk costumes. 256pp. 8⅜ x 11¾. 0-486-23150-X

MATHEMATICS FOR THE NONMATHEMATICIAN, Morris Kline. Detailed, college-level treatment of mathematics in cultural and historical context, with numerous exercises. Recommended Reading Lists. Tables. Numerous figures. 641pp. 5⅜ x 8½. 0-486-24823-2

PROBABILISTIC METHODS IN THE THEORY OF STRUCTURES, Isaac Elishakoff. Well-written introduction covers the elements of the theory of probability from two or more random variables, the reliability of such multivariable structures, the theory of random function, Monte Carlo methods of treating problems incapable of exact solution, and more. Examples. 502pp. 5⅜ x 8½. 0-486-40691-1

THE RIME OF THE ANCIENT MARINER, Gustave Doré, S. T. Coleridge. Doré's finest work; 34 plates capture moods, subtleties of poem. Flawless full-size reproductions printed on facing pages with authoritative text of poem. "Beautiful. Simply beautiful."–*Publisher's Weekly.* 77pp. 9¼ x 12. 0-486-22305-1

SCULPTURE: Principles and Practice, Louis Slobodkin. Step-by-step approach to clay, plaster, metals, stone; classical and modern. 253 drawings, photos. 255pp. 8⅛ x 11. 0-486-22960-2

THE INFLUENCE OF SEA POWER UPON HISTORY, 1660–1783, A. T. Mahan. Influential classic of naval history and tactics still used as text in war colleges. First paperback edition. 4 maps. 24 battle plans. 640pp. 5⅜ x 8½. 0-486-25509-3

THE STORY OF THE TITANIC AS TOLD BY ITS SURVIVORS, Jack Winocour (ed.). What it was really like. Panic, despair, shocking inefficiency, and a little heroism. More thrilling than any fictional account. 26 illustrations. 320pp. 5⅜ x 8½. 0-486-20610-6

ONE TWO THREE . . . INFINITY: Facts and Speculations of Science, George Gamow. Great physicist's fascinating, readable overview of contemporary science: number theory, relativity, fourth dimension, entropy, genes, atomic structure, much more. 128 illustrations. Index. 352pp. 5⅜ x 8½. 0-486-25664-2

DALÍ ON MODERN ART: The Cuckolds of Antiquated Modern Art, Salvador Dalí. Influential painter skewers modern art and its practitioners. Outrageous evaluations of Picasso, Cézanne, Turner, more. 15 renderings of paintings discussed. 44 calligraphic decorations by Dalí. 96pp. 5⅜ x 8½. (Available in U.S. only.) 0-486-29220-7

ANTIQUE PLAYING CARDS: A Pictorial History, Henry René D'Allemagne. Over 900 elaborate, decorative images from rare playing cards (14th–20th centuries): Bacchus, death, dancing dogs, hunting scenes, royal coats of arms, players cheating, much more. 96pp. 9¼ x 12¼. 0-486-29265-7

CATALOG OF DOVER BOOKS

MAKING FURNITURE MASTERPIECES: 30 Projects with Measured Drawings, Franklin H. Gottshall. Step-by-step instructions, illustrations for constructing handsome, useful pieces, among them a Sheraton desk, Chippendale chair, Spanish desk, Queen Anne table and a William and Mary dressing mirror. 224pp. 8⅛ x 11¼.
0-486-29338-6

NORTH AMERICAN INDIAN DESIGNS FOR ARTISTS AND CRAFTSPEOPLE, Eva Wilson. Over 360 authentic copyright-free designs adapted from Navajo blankets, Hopi pottery, Sioux buffalo hides, more. Geometrics, symbolic figures, plant and animal motifs, etc. 128pp. 8⅜ x 11. (Not for sale in the United Kingdom.) 0-486-25341-4

THE FOSSIL BOOK: A Record of Prehistoric Life, Patricia V. Rich et al. Profusely illustrated definitive guide covers everything from single-celled organisms and dinosaurs to birds and mammals and the interplay between climate and man. Over 1,500 illustrations. 760pp. 7½ x 10⅛. 0-486-29371-8

VICTORIAN ARCHITECTURAL DETAILS: Designs for Over 700 Stairs, Mantels, Doors, Windows, Cornices, Porches, and Other Decorative Elements, A. J. Bicknell & Company. Everything from dormer windows and piazzas to balconies and gable ornaments. Also includes elevations and floor plans for handsome, private residences and commercial structures. 80pp. 9⅜ x 12¼. 0-486-44015-X

WESTERN ISLAMIC ARCHITECTURE: A Concise Introduction, John D. Hoag. Profusely illustrated critical appraisal compares and contrasts Islamic mosques and palaces—from Spain and Egypt to other areas in the Middle East. 139 illustrations. 128pp. 6 x 9. 0-486-43760-4

CHINESE ARCHITECTURE: A Pictorial History, Liang Ssu-ch'eng. More than 240 rare photographs and drawings depict temples, pagodas, tombs, bridges, and imperial palaces comprising much of China's architectural heritage. 152 halftones, 94 diagrams. 232pp. 10¾ x 9⅞. 0-486-43999-2

THE RENAISSANCE: Studies in Art and Poetry, Walter Pater. One of the most talked-about books of the 19th century, *The Renaissance* combines scholarship and philosophy in an innovative work of cultural criticism that examines the achievements of Botticelli, Leonardo, Michelangelo, and other artists. "The holy writ of beauty."—Oscar Wilde. 160pp. 5⅜ x 8½. 0-486-44025-7

A TREATISE ON PAINTING, Leonardo da Vinci. The great Renaissance artist's practical advice on drawing and painting techniques covers anatomy, perspective, composition, light and shadow, and color. A classic of art instruction, it features 48 drawings by Nicholas Poussin and Leon Battista Alberti. 192pp. 5⅜ x 8½.
0-486-44155-5

THE MIND OF LEONARDO DA VINCI, Edward McCurdy. More than just a biography, this classic study by a distinguished historian draws upon Leonardo's extensive writings to offer numerous demonstrations of the Renaissance master's achievements, not only in sculpture and painting, but also in music, engineering, and even experimental aviation. 384pp. 5⅜ x 8½. 0-486-44142-3

WASHINGTON IRVING'S RIP VAN WINKLE, Illustrated by Arthur Rackham. Lovely prints that established artist as a leading illustrator of the time and forever etched into the popular imagination a classic of Catskill lore. 51 full-color plates. 80pp. 8⅜ x 11. 0-486-44242-X

HENSCHE ON PAINTING, John W. Robichaux. Basic painting philosophy and methodology of a great teacher, as expounded in his famous classes and workshops on Cape Cod. 7 illustrations in color on covers. 80pp. 5⅜ x 8½. 0-486-43728-0

LIGHT AND SHADE: A Classic Approach to Three-Dimensional Drawing, Mrs. Mary P. Merrifield. Handy reference clearly demonstrates principles of light and shade by revealing effects of common daylight, sunshine, and candle or artificial light on geometrical solids. 13 plates. 64pp. 5⅜ x 8½. 0-486-44143-1

ASTROLOGY AND ASTRONOMY: A Pictorial Archive of Signs and Symbols, Ernst and Johanna Lehner. Treasure trove of stories, lore, and myth, accompanied by more than 300 rare illustrations of planets, the Milky Way, signs of the zodiac, comets, meteors, and other astronomical phenomena. 192pp. 8⅜ x 11. 0-486-43981-X

JEWELRY MAKING: Techniques for Metal, Tim McCreight. Easy-to-follow instructions and carefully executed illustrations describe tools and techniques, use of gems and enamels, wire inlay, casting, and other topics. 72 line illustrations and diagrams. 176pp. 8¼ x 10⅞. 0-486-44043-5

MAKING BIRDHOUSES: Easy and Advanced Projects, Gladstone Califf. Easy-to-follow instructions include diagrams for everything from a one-room house for bluebirds to a forty-two-room structure for purple martins. 56 plates; 4 figures. 80pp. 8¾ x 6⅜. 0-486-44183-0

LITTLE BOOK OF LOG CABINS: How to Build and Furnish Them, William S. Wicks. Handy how-to manual, with instructions and illustrations for building cabins in the Adirondack style, fireplaces, stairways, furniture, beamed ceilings, and more. 102 line drawings. 96pp. 8¾ x 6⅜. 0-486-44259-4

THE SEASONS OF AMERICA PAST, Eric Sloane. From "sugaring time" and strawberry picking to Indian summer and fall harvest, a whole year's activities described in charming prose and enhanced with 79 of the author's own illustrations. 160pp. 8¼ x 11. 0-486-44220-9

THE METROPOLIS OF TOMORROW, Hugh Ferriss. Generous, prophetic vision of the metropolis of the future, as perceived in 1929. Powerful illustrations of towering structures, wide avenues, and rooftop parks–all features in many of today's modern cities. 59 illustrations. 144pp. 8¼ x 11. 0-486-43727-2

THE PATH TO ROME, Hilaire Belloc. This 1902 memoir abounds in lively vignettes from a vanished time, recounting a pilgrimage on foot across the Alps and Apennines in order to "see all Europe which the Christian Faith has saved." 77 of the author's original line drawings complement his sparkling prose. 272pp. 5⅜ x 8½. 0-486-44001-X

THE HISTORY OF RASSELAS: Prince of Abissinia, Samuel Johnson. Distinguished English writer attacks eighteenth-century optimism and man's unrealistic estimates of what life has to offer. 112pp. 5⅜ x 8½. 0-486-44094-X

A VOYAGE TO ARCTURUS, David Lindsay. A brilliant flight of pure fancy, where wild creatures crowd the fantastic landscape and demented torturers dominate victims with their bizarre mental powers. 272pp. 5⅜ x 8½. 0-486-44198-9

Paperbound unless otherwise indicated. Available at your book dealer, online at **www.doverpublications.com**, or by writing to Dept. GI, Dover Publications, Inc., 31 East 2nd Street, Mineola, NY 11501. For current price information or for free catalogs (please indicate field of interest), write to Dover Publications or log on to **www.doverpublications.com** and see every Dover book in print. Dover publishes more than 500 books each year on science, elementary and advanced mathematics, biology, music, art, literary history, social sciences, and other areas.